FAMOUS CULTURAL SITES OF INDIA

EVERYTHING ABOUT CULTURAL SITES OF INDIA

ANKIT YADAV

Made with ♥ on the Notion Press Platform
www.notionpress.com

Dedicated to all my friends..

Contents

PREFACE

I want whole world to know about India's rich cultural sites. If you want to know India better both through dark and bright side of India's cultural sites you must read this book.

Indian heritage dates back several centuries. It is vast and vibrant. Flora and fauna, music, architecture, classical dance, and the innate secular philosophy of its people are the highlights of India's treasure. Ever since the beginning, we have preserved culture and tradition beautifully for our upcoming generations. We can never forget our tradition and culture as they are embedded in us and are an inseparable part of our lives no matter how far we plan to reach and how much we have progressed in all these years.

In India, people from numerous religious castes and creeds reside in the same country and so it is the land of diversified cultures and traditions. Each religion and caste has its own traditions and Customs. Each religious group follows the culture and has a deep unwavering faith and underlying roots.

We take pride in our heritage and we also have a magnification of monumental Heritage. Most of the beautiful edifices exhibit a royal past that was built by the rulers and still stands tall. Let's talk about it.

PREFACE

I want whole world to know about India's [illegible] sites. If you want to know India better both through dark and bright side of India's cultural sites you must read this book.

Indian heritage [illegible] been [illegible] and vibrant. [illegible] dance, and [illegible] the highlights of [illegible] ever since the beginning, we have preserved culture and tradition [illegible] for our upcoming generations. We [illegible] and culture [illegible] embedded in [illegible] inseparable part of our [illegible] reach and [illegible]

In [illegible] and [illegible] of diversified cultures and traditions. [illegible] religion and caste has its own traditions and [illegible] group follows the culture and has a deep [illegible] faith and underlying roots.

We take pride in our heritage [illegible] magnification of [illegible] beautiful edifices exhibit [illegible] rulers and [illegible]

ACKNOWLEDGEMENTS

Writing a book is harder than I thought and more rewarding than I could have ever imagined. None of this would have been possible without the help from Shiv Nadar Foundation(Vidya Gyan School)

Shiv Nadar Sir(Chairperson of HCL Enterprizes)

Roshini Nadar(Chaiperson of HCL Technologies)

Capt.Vijay Tewari(Administarator VidyaGyan School)

Swati S Saligram (Principal VidyaGyan School Sitapur)

Ramesh Kumar Bajpayee (Chairperson Sita Group Of Education Mahmudabad Sitapur)

I'm eternally grateful to my teacher Barbara Burder Ma'am who always helped me in developing the writing skills.Thank you so much ma'am ..

I thank to all my teachers ....

To my family, to my mother for always being the person I can turn to during the dark and desperate times. She sustaine me in ways that I never know that I needed. Thanks to my brothers who always helped me emotionally and financially.

Finally, to all those who have been a part of my getting there.

Thanks to all my Freinds

ARYAN PRATAP SINGH

SHASHANK VERMA

SHIVAM YADAV

AKHAY SHUKLA

AYUSH VERMA

AYUSHI SINGH

SHUBHI SINGH

ABHISHEK VERMA
ANSHIKA PATEL
SAPNA YADAV
AASTHA YADAV
AMIT SHUKLA
ANIKET KUMAR
ANURADHA KUMARI
AVANISH JAISWAL
KHUSHI GUPTA
KUMARI KOMAL
NITESH KUMAR
PRANAY GUPTA
RAHUL KUMAR CHAUHAN
RAJAN KASAUDHAN
RAJEEV KUMAR
SATYAM GUPTA
SHAURYA PRATAP SINGH
SURAJ UPADHYAY
VISHAL VERMA
VIVEKANAND YADAV
AMIT KUMAR SHUKLA
ANKIT SINGH
ANSH SHUKLA
ANSHIKA SHARMA
ARADHYA VERMA
ARPITA GUPTA
DHANANJAY SINGH
KRISHNANAND MISHRA
MANGESH SONI
RAGINI TIWARI
RAJAN JAISWAL
RAM KRISHNA
ROSHNI CHAURASIYA

SAMEERATMAJ
SAUJANYABAJPAI
SHIKHABAJPAI
SRIJAN
TARUNIMA SINGH
AAKASH GUPTA
ABHISHEK SHUKLA
ADVIKA SINGH
ALOK YADAV
AYUSHI YADAV
GEETA YADAV
KUSHAL SHARMA
KHUSHBOO YADAV
LAKSHMI
MUSKAN JAISWAL
NAITIK YADAV
NIMISHA GUPTA
SAURABH VERMA
SHAILAJA AWASTHI
SHIVENDRA YADAV
SURAJ KUMAR
VINEET YADAV
VIVEK VERMA
AJAY PAL
AKASH VERMA
AKASH SINGH
AMAN MADHESIYA
ARYA PRATAP SINGH
DIPTIPRABHA GUPTA
DIVYANSHI CHAURASIYA
NIKITA TIWARI
PRABHAT MAURYA
RAJ DWIVEDI

RUPESH KUMAR
SAKSHI DIXIT
SAUJANYA SHUKLA
SHISHIR YADAV
SHLOK YADAV
VIKAS YADAV
YUVRAJ VERMA
SHAYER NEERAJ YADAV
SHUBHAM SINGH YADAV
SACHIN YADAV
ANOOP YADAV
PANKAJ YADAV
SUBODH KUMAR
DEEPANASHU
PALLAVI
DHARMENDRA KUMAR
MOHIT YADAV
ANKIT KUMAR
SUNEEL KUMAR YADAV
...THANKS TO ALL...

Prologue

Cultural heritage has the potential to promote access to and enjoyment of cultural diversity. It can also enrich social capital and create a sense of individual and collective belonging, which helps to maintain social and territorial cohesion.

Conservation of Heritage sites in India is important because: Conservation of heritage sites and buildings provides a sense of identity and continuity in a fast-changing world. Heritage sites and buildings represent the past history and culture of a nation. It is important to support the tourism industry. Indian culture is based on respect for elders, family unity, honesty, and hard work. Indian values also emphasize education, both formal and informal. India is a land of great opportunity, and its citizens are known for their entrepreneurial spirit.

I

Taj Mahal

The Taj Mahal ('Crown of the Palace') is an Islamic ivory-white marble mausoleum on the right bank of the river Yamuna in the Indian city of Agra. It was commissioned in 1631 by the Mughal emperor Shah Jahan (r. 1628–1658) to house the tomb of his favorite wife, Mumtaz Mahal; it also houses the tomb of Shah Jahan himself. The tomb is the centerpiece of a 17-hectare (42-acre) complex, which includes a mosque and a guest house, and is set in formal gardens bounded on three sides by a crenellated wall.

Construction of the mausoleum was essentially completed in 1643, but work continued on other phases of the project for another 10 years. The Taj Mahal complex is believed to have been completed in its entirety in 1653 at a cost estimated at the time to be around ?32 million, which in 2020 would be approximately ?70 billion (about US $1 billion). The construction project employed some 20,000 artisans under the guidance of a board of architects led by Ustad Ahmad Lahauri, the emperor's court architect. Various types of symbolism have been employed in the Taj to reflect natural beauty and divinity.

The Taj Mahal was designated as a UNESCO World Heritage Site in 1983 for being "the jewel of Muslim art in India and one of the universally admired masterpieces of the world's heritage". It is regarded by many as the best example of Mughal architecture and a symbol of India's rich history. The Taj Mahal attracts more than 6 million visitors a year and in 2007, it was declared a winner of the New 7 Wonders of the World (2000–2007) initiative.

Inspiration

The Taj Mahal was commissioned by Shah Jahan in 1631, to be built in the memory of his wife Mumtaz Mahal, who died on 17 June that year, while giving birth to their 14th child, Gauhara Begum. Construction started in 1632, and the mausoleum was completed in 1648, while the surrounding buildings and garden were finished five years later. The imperial court documenting Shah Jahan's grief after the death of Mumtaz Mahal illustrates the love story held as the inspiration for the Taj Mahal

The Taj Mahal incorporates and expands on design traditions of Indo-Islamic and earlier Mughal architecture. Specific inspiration came from successful Timurid and Mughal buildings including the Gur-e Amir (The tomb of Timur, progenitor of the Mughal dynasty, in Samarkand),[17] Humayun's Tomb which inspired the Charbagh gardens and hasht-behesht (architecture) plan of the site, Itmad-Ud-Daulah's Tomb (sometimes called the Baby Taj), and Shah Jahan's own Jama Masjid in Delhi. While earlier Mughal buildings were primarily constructed of red sandstone, Shah Jahan promoted the use of white marble inlaid with semi-precious stones. Buildings under his patronage reached new levels of refinement.

Tomb

The tomb is the central focus of the entire complex of the Taj Mahal. It is a large, white marble structure standing on a square plinth and consists of a symmetrical building with an iwan (an arch-shaped doorway) topped by a large dome and finial. Like most Mughal tombs, the basic elements are Indo-Islamic in origin.[19]

The base structure is a large multi-chambered cube with chamfered corners forming an unequal eight-sided structure about 55 meters (180 ft) on each of the four long sides. Each side of the Iwan is framed with a huge pishtaq or vaulted archway with two similarly shaped arched balconies stacked on either side. This motif of stacked pishtaqs is replicated on the chamfered corner areas, making the design completely symmetrical on all sides of the building. Four minarets frame the tomb, one at each corner of the plinth facing the chamfered corners. The main chamber houses the false sarcophagi of Mumtaz Mahal and Shah Jahan; the actual graves are at a lower level

The most spectacular feature is the marble dome that surmounts the tomb. The dome is nearly 35 metres (115 ft) high, close to the base's length, and accentuated by the cylindrical "drum" it sits on, which is about 7 meters (23 ft) high. Because of its shape, the dome is often called an onion dome or amrud (guava dome). The top is decorated with a lotus design which also serves to accentuate its height. The shape of the dome is emphasized by four smaller domed chattris (kiosks) placed at its corners, which replicate the onion shape of the main dome. The dome is slightly asymmetrical. Their columned bases open through the roof of the tomb and provide light to the interior. Tall decorative spires (guldastas) extend from edges of base walls and provide visual emphasis to the dome's height. The lotus motif is repeated on both the chattris and guldastas. The dome and chattris are topped by a gilded finial which mixes traditional Persian and Hindustani decorative elements.

The main finial was originally made of gold but was replaced by a copy made of gilded bronze in the early 19th century. This feature provides a clear example of integration of traditional Persian and Hindu decorative elements. The finial is topped by a moon, a typical Islamic motif whose horns point heavenward.

The minarets, which are each more than 40 metres (130 ft) tall, display the designer's penchant for symmetry. They were designed as working minarets— a traditional element of mosques, used by the muezzin to call the Islamic faithful to prayer. Each minaret is effectively divided into three equal parts by two working balconies that ring the tower. At the top of the tower is a final balcony surmounted by a chattri that mirrors the design of those on the tomb. The chattris all share the same decorative elements of a lotus design topped by a gilded finial. The minarets were constructed slightly outside of the plinth so that in the event of collapse, a typical occurrence with many tall constructions of the period, the material from the towers would tend to fall away from the tomb.

Exterior decorations

The exterior decorations of the Taj Mahal are among the finest in Mughal architecture. As the surface area changes, the decorations are refined proportionally. The decorative elements were created by applying paint, stucco, stone inlays, or carvings. In line with the Islamic prohibition against the use of anthropomorphic forms, the decorative elements can be grouped into either calligraphy, abstract forms, or vegetative motifs. Throughout the complex are passages from the Qur'an that comprise some of the decorative elements. Recent scholarship suggests that

Amanat Khan chose the passages.

The calligraphy on the Great Gate reads "O Soul, thou art at rest. Return to the Lord at peace with Him, and He at peace with you."The calligraphy was created in 1609 by a calligrapher named Abdul Haq. Shah Jahan conferred the title of "Amanat Khan" upon him as a reward for his "dazzling virtuosity".Near the lines from the Qur'an at the base of the interior dome is the inscription, "Written by the insignificant being, Amanat Khan Shirazi."Much of the calligraphy is composed of florid thuluth script made of jasper or black marble inlaid in white marble panels. Higher panels are written in slightly larger script to reduce the skewing effect when viewed from below. The calligraphy found on the marble cenotaphs in the tomb is particularly detailed and delicate.

Abstract forms are used throughout, especially in the plinth, minarets, gateway, mosque, jawab and, to a lesser extent, on the surfaces of the tomb. The domes and vaults of the sandstone buildings are worked with tracery of incised painting to create elaborate geometric forms. Herringbone inlays define the space between many of the adjoining elements. White inlays are used in sandstone buildings, and dark or black inlays on the white marbles. Mortared areas of the marble buildings have been stained or painted in a contrasting colour which creates a complex array of geometric patterns. Floors and walkways use contrasting tiles or blocks in tessellation patterns.

On the lower walls of the tomb are white marble dados sculpted with realistic bas relief depictions of flowers and vines. The marble has been polished to emphasise the exquisite detailing of the carvings. The dado frames and archway spandrels have been decorated with pietra dura inlays of highly stylised, almost geometric vines, flowers, and fruits. The inlay stones are of yellow marble, jasper, and jade, polished and levelled to the surface of the walls.

The Taj Mahal complex is bordered on three sides by crenellated red sandstone walls; the side facing the river is open. Outside the walls are several additional mausoleums, including those of Shah Jahan's other wives, and a larger tomb for Mumtaz's favourite servant.These structures, composed primarily of red sandstone, are typical of the smaller Mughal tombs of the era. The garden-facing inner sides of the wall are fronted by columned arcades, a feature typical of Hindu temples which was later incorporated into Mughal mosques. The wall is interspersed with domed chattris, and small buildings that may have been viewing areas or watch towers like the Music House, which is now used as a museum.

The main gateway (darwaza) is a monumental structure built primarily of marble, and reminiscent of the Mughal architecture of earlier emperors. Its archways mirror the shape of the tomb's archways, and its pishtaq arches incorporate the calligraphy that decorates the tomb. It utilises bas-relief and pietra dura inlaid decorations with floral motifs. The vaulted ceilings and walls have elaborate geometric designs like those found in the other sandstone buildings in the complex.

At the far end of the complex are two grand red sandstone buildings that mirror each other, and face the sides of the tomb. The backs of the buildings parallel the western and eastern walls. The western building is a mosque and the other is the jawab (answer), thought to have been constructed for architectural balance although it may have been used as a guesthouse. Distinctions between the two buildings include the jawab's lack of a mihrab (a niche in a mosque's wall facing Mecca), and its floors of geometric design whereas the floor of the mosque is laid with outlines of 569 prayer rugs in black marble. The mosque's basic design of a long hall surmounted by three domes is similar to others built by Shah Jahan, particularly the Masjid-i Jahān-Numā, or Jama Masjid, Delhi. The Mughal mosques of this period divide the sanctuary hall into three areas comprising a main sanctuary and slightly smaller sanctuaries on either side. At the Taj Mahal, each sanctuary opens onto an expansive vaulting dome. The outlying buildings were completed in 1643.

Construction

The Taj Mahal is built on a parcel of land to the south of the walled city of Agra. Shah Jahan presented Maharaja Jai Singh I with a large palace in the centre of Agra in exchange for the land.An area of roughly 1.2 hectares (3 acres) was excavated, filled with dirt to reduce seepage, and levelled at 50 metres (160 ft) above the riverbank level. In the tomb area, piles were dug and filled with stone and rubble to form the footings of the tomb. Instead of lashed bamboo, workmen constructed a colossal brick scaffold that mirrored the tomb. The scaffold was so enormous that foremen expected it to take years to dismantle.

The Taj Mahal was constructed using materials from all over India and Asia. It is believed over 1,000 elephants were used to transport building materials. Some 22,000 labourers, painters, embroidery artists and stonecutters were used. The translucent white marble was brought from Makrana, Rajasthan, the jasper from the Punjab region, jade and crystal from China. The turquoise was from Tibet and the Lapis lazuli from Afghanistan, while the sapphire came from Sri Lanka and the carnelian from Arabia. In all, 28 types of precious and semi-precious stone were inlaid into the white marble.

According to the legend, Shah Jahan decreed that anyone could keep the bricks taken from the scaffold, and thus it was dismantled by peasants overnight.A 15-kilometre (9.3 mi) tamped-earth ramp was built to transport marble and materials to the construction site and teams of 20 or 30 oxen pulled the blocks on specially constructed wagons.An elaborate post-and-beam pulley system was used to raise the blocks into the desired position. Water was drawn from the river by a series of purs, an animal-powered rope and bucket mechanism, into a large storage tank and raised to a large distribution tank. It was passed into three subsidiary tanks, from which it was piped to the complex.

The plinth and tomb took some 12 years to complete. The remaining parts of the complex took an additional 10 years and were completed in order of minarets, mosque and jawab, and gateway. Since the complex was built in stages, discrepancies exist in completion dates due to differing opinions on "completion". Construction of the mausoleum was completed by 1643 while work on the outlying buildings continued for years. Estimates of the cost of construction vary due to difficulties in estimating costs across time. The total cost at the time has been estimated to be about ? 32 million,which is around ? 52.8 billion ($827 million US) based on 2015 values.

Symbolism

Due to the global attention that it has received and the millions of visitors it attracts, the Taj Mahal has become a prominent image that is associated with India, and in this way has become a symbol of India itself.

Along with being a renowned symbol of love, the Taj Mahal is also a symbol of Shah Jahan's wealth and power, and the fact that the empire had prospered under his rule.Bilateral symmetry dominated by a central axis has been used by rulers as a symbol of a ruling force that brings balance and harmony, and Shah Jahan applied that concept in the making of the Taj Mahal.Additionally, the plan is aligned in the cardinal north–south direction and the corners have been placed so that when seen from the center of the plan, the sun can be seen rising and setting on the north and south corners on the summer and winter solstices respectively. This makes the Taj a symbolic horizon.

The planning and structure of the Taj Mahal, from the building to the gardens and beyond, symbolizes Mumtaz Mahal's mansion in the garden of Paradise. The concept of Gardens of Paradise is extended into the mausoleum building too. Colorful vines and flowers decorate the interior, and are filled in with semi-precious stones using a technique called pietra dura, or as the Mughals called it, parchin kari.The building appears to slightly change color depending on the time of day and the weather. The sky has been incorporated in the design through the reflecting pools and through the building's surface. This is another way to imply the presence of Allah at the site.

According to Ebba Koch, art historian and international expert in the understanding and interpretation of Mughal architecture and the Taj Mahal, the planning of the entire compound of the Taj symbolizes earthly life and the afterlife, a subset of the symbolization of the divine. The plan has been split into two—one half is the white marble mausoleum itself and the gardens, and the other half is the red sandstone side meant for worldly markets. Only the mausoleum is white to represent the enlightenment, spirituality and faith of Mumtaz Mahal. According to the world-traveler Eleanor Roosevelt, the white symbolized the purity of real love.Koch has deciphered that symbolic of Islamic teachings, the plan of the worldly side is a mirror image of the otherworldly side, and the grand gate in the middle represents the transition between the two lives.

The Taj is also seen as a feminine architectural form, and is thought to embody Mumtaz Mahal herself.

Later days

Soon after the Taj Mahal's completion, Shah Jahan was deposed by his son Aurangzeb and put under house arrest at nearby Agra Fort. Upon Shah Jahan's death, Aurangzeb buried him in the mausoleum next to his wife. In the 18th century, the Jat rulers of Bharatpur invaded Agra and attacked the Taj Mahal. They took away the two chandeliers, one of agate and another of silver, which were hung over the main cenotaph; they also took the gold and silver screen. Kanbo, a Mughal historian, said the gold shield which covered the 4.6-metre-high (15 ft) finial at the top of the main dome was also removed during the Jat despoliation.

By the late 19th century, parts of the buildings had fallen into disrepair. At the end of the 19th century, British viceroy Lord Curzon ordered a sweeping restoration project, which was completed in 1908.He also commissioned the large lamp in the interior chamber, modelled after one in a Cairo mosque. During this time, the garden was remodelled with European-style lawns still in place.

Threats

Protective wartime scaffolding in 1942

In 1942, the government erected scaffolding to disguise the building in anticipation of air attacks by the Japanese Air Force.During the India-Pakistan wars of 1965 and 1971, scaffolding was again erected to mislead bomber pilots.

More recent threats have come from environmental pollution on the banks of the Yamuna River including acid rain due to the Mathura Oil Refinery, which was opposed by Supreme Court of India directives. The pollution has been turning the Taj Mahal yellow-brown. To help control the pollution, the Indian government has set up the "Taj Trapezium Zone (TTZ)", a 10,400-square-kilometre (4,000 sq mi) area around the monument where strict emissions standards are in place.

Concerns for the tomb's structural integrity have recently been raised because of a decline in the groundwater level in the Yamuna river basin which is falling at a rate of around 1.5 m (5 ft) per year. In 2010, cracks appeared in parts of the tomb, and the minarets which surround the monument were showing signs of tilting, as the wooden foundation of the tomb may be rotting due to lack of water. It has been pointed out by politicians, however, that the minarets are designed to tilt slightly outwards to prevent them from crashing on top of the tomb in the event of an earthquake. In 2011, it was reported that some predictions indicated that the tomb could collapse within five years.

Small minarets located at two of the outlying buildings were reported as damaged by a storm on April 11, 2018. On 31 May 2020 another fierce thunderstorm caused some damage to the complex.

Tourism

Visitors at Taj Mahal

The Taj Mahal attracts many tourists. UNESCO documented more than 2 million visitors in 2001,which had increased to about 7–8 million in 2014. A three-tier pricing system is in place, with a significantly lower entrance fee for Indian citizens and more expensive ones for foreigners.

As of 2022, the fee for Indian citizens was ?50, for citizens of SAARC and BIMSTEC countries ?540, for foreign tourists ?1,100.[73] Most tourists visit in the cooler months of October, November, and February. Polluting traffic is not allowed near the complex and tourists must either walk from parking areas or catch an electric bus. The Khawasspuras (northern courtyards) are being restored as a new visitor centre.In 2019, to address overtourism, the site instituted fines for visitors who stayed longer than three hours.

The small town to the south of the Taj, known as Taj Ganji or Mumtazabad, was initially constructed with caravanserais, bazaars and markets to serve the needs of visitors and workers.Lists of recommended travel destinations often feature the Taj Mahal, which also appears in several listings of seven wonders of the modern world, including the recently announced New Seven Wonders of the World, a recent poll with 100 million votes.

The grounds are open from 06:00 to 19:00 weekdays, except for Friday when the complex is open for prayers at the mosque between 12:00 and 14:00. The complex is open for night viewing on the day of the full moon and two days before and after,excluding Fridays and the month of Ramadan.

II

Jal Mahal

In the center of Man Sagar Lake in Jaipur, the Indian state of Rajasthan's capital, sits a palace called Jal Mahal, which translates to "Water Palace." The palace was initially built in 1699, and Maharaja Jai Singh II of Amber later rebuilt and expanded the structure and the lake surrounding it.

The Jal Mahal palace is an architectural showcase of the Rajput style of architecture (common in Rajasthan) on a grand scale. The building has a picturesque view of Man Sagar Lake, but owing to its seclusion from land is equally the focus of a viewpoint from the Man Sagar Dam on the eastern side of the lake in front of the backdrop of the surrounding Nahargarh ("tiger-abode") hills. The palace, built in red sandstone, is a five-storied building, of which four floors remain underwater when the lake is full and the top floor is expose. One rectangular Chhatri on the roof is of the Bengal type. The chhatris on the four corners are octagonal. The palace had suffered subsidence in the past and also partial seepage (plaster work and wall damage equivalent to rising damp) because of water logging, which have been repaired under a restoration project of the

Government of Rajasthan.

The hills surrounding the lake area, towards the north east of Jaipur, have quartzite rock formations (with a thin layer of soil cover), which is part of the Aravalli hills range. Rock exposures on the surface in some parts of the project area have also been used for constructing buildings. From the northeast, the Kanak Vrindavan valley, where a temple complex sits, the hills slope gently towards the lake edge. Within the lake area, the ground area is made up of a thick mantle of soil, blown sand, and alluvium. Forest denudation, particularly in the hilly areas, has caused soil erosion, compounded by wind and water action. As a result, silt built up in the lake incrementally raises the lake bed. On the terrace of the palace, a garden was built with arched passages. At each corner of this palace semi-octagonal towers were built with an elegant cupola.

The restoration works of the early 2000s were not satisfactory and an expert in the field of similar architectural restoration works of Rajasthan palaces examined the designs that could decipher the originally existing designs on the walls, after removing the recent plasterwork. Based on this finding, restoration works were re-done with traditional materials for plastering – the plaster consists of partly organic material: a mortar mix of lime, sand and surkhi mixed with jaggery, guggal and methi powder. It was also noticed that there was hardly any water seepage, except for a little dampness, on the floors below the water level. But the original garden, which existed on the terrace had been lost. Now, a new terrace is being created based on a similar roof garden of the Amer Palace.The building is located near the shoreline of a lake with a maximum depth of 15 ft. As the four stories of the building are built under the water, this means it would be structured on the bottom of the lake.

III

Lotus Temple

The Lotus Temple, located in Delhi, India, is a Bahai House of Worship that was dedicated in December 1986. Notable for its lotuslike shape, it has become a prominent attraction in the city. Like all other Bahá'í Houses of Worship, the Lotus Temple is open to all, regardless of religion or any other qualification. The building is composed of 27 free-standing marble-clad "petals" arranged in clusters of three to form nine sides with nine doors opening onto a central hall with a height of slightly over 34 meters and a capacity of 1,300 people. The Lotus Temple has won numerous architectural awards and has been featured in many newspaper and magazine articles.

History

The architect of the Lotus Temple was an Iranian, Fariborz Sahba who now lives in La Jolla, California, after living some years in Canada.He was approached in 1976 to design the Lotus Temple and later oversaw its construction. The structural design was undertaken by the UK firm Flint and Neill over the course of 18 months (about 1 and a half years), and the construction was done by ECC Construction

Group of Larsen & Toubro Limite at a cost of $10 million.The major part of the funds needed to buy this land was donated by Ardishír Rustampúr of Hyderabad, Sindh (Pakistan), whose will dictated that his entire life savings would go to this purpose A portion of the construction budget was saved and used to build a greenhouse to study indigenous plants and flowers that would be appropriate for use on the site.

Ruhiyyih Khanum laid the foundation stone for the Lotus Temple on 19 October 1977 and dedicated the temple on 24 December 1986.For the dedication, there was a gathering of 8,000 Bahá'ís from 107 countries, including some 4,000 Bahais from 22 provinces in India. The temple was opened to the public on 1 January 1987 and more than 10,000 people visited that day.

Worship

The Bahá'í Faith teaches that a Bahá'í House of Worship should be a space for people of all religions to gather, reflect, and worship.Anyone may enter the Lotus Temple irrespective of religious background, gender, or other distinctions, as is the case with all Bahá'í Houses of Worship. The sacred writings of not only the Bahá'í Faith but also other religions can be read and/or chanted, regardless of language; on the other hand, reading nonscriptural texts is forbidden, as are delivering sermons or lectures, or fundraising. Musical renditions of readings and prayers can be sung by choirs, but no musical instruments can be played inside. There is no set pattern for worship services, and ritualistic ceremonies are not permitted.

Structure

All Bahá'í Houses of Worship, including the Lotus Temple, share certain architectural elements, some of which are specified by Bahá'í scripture. 'Abdu'l-Bahá, the son of the founder of the religion, wrote that Bahá'í Houses of Worship must be nine-sided and circular. While all current Bahá'í Houses of Worship have a dome, this is not regarded as an essential part of their architecture. Bahá'í scripture also states that no pictures, statues or images be displayed within the House of Worship and no pulpits or altars be incorporated as an architectural feature (readers may stand behind simple portable lecture stands).

Inspired by the lotus flower, the design for the House of Worship in New Delhi is composed of 27 free-standing marble-clad "petals" arranged in clusters of three to form nine sides. The temple's shape has symbolic and inter-religious significance because the lotus is often associated with purity, sacredness, spirituality and knowledge. It has a spiritual significance in India. The nine doors of the Lotus Temple open onto a central hall 34.3 meters tall that can seat 1,300 people and hold up to 2,500 in all.The temple has a diameter of 70 m. The surface of the House of Worship is made of white marble from Penteli mountain in Greece, the same marble used in the construction of many ancient monuments (including the Parthenon) and other Bahá'í buildings. Along with its nine surrounding ponds and gardens, the Lotus Temple property comprises 26 acres (105,000 m^2; 10.5 ha). An educational centre beside the temple was established in 2017.

The Lotus Temple is situated near Okhla NSIC and Kalkaji Mandir metro station is just 500 meters away.It is in the village of Bahapur in New Delhi, National Capital Territory of Delhi, near Nehru Place.

Of the temple's total electricity use of 500 kilowatts (kW), 120 kW is provided by solar power generated by solar panels on the building. This saves the temple ?120,000 per month.It is the first temple in Delhi to use solar power.

As is the case with other stone monuments such as the Taj Mahal, the Lotus Temple is becoming discolored due to air pollution in India. Specifically, the white marble is turning grey and yellow due to pollution from vehicles and manufacturing in the city, among other sources.

IV

Elephanta Caves

The 'City of Caves', on an island in the Sea of Oman close to Bombay, contains a collection of rock art linked to the cult of Shiva. Here, Indian art has found one of its most perfect expressions, particularly the huge high reliefs in the main cave.

Brief synthesis

The Elephanta Caves are located in Western India on Elephanta Island (otherwise known as the Island of Gharapuri), which features two hillocks separated by a narrow valley. The small island is dotted with numerous ancient archaeological remains that are the sole testimonies to its rich cultural past. These archaeological remains reveal evidence of occupation from as early as the 2nd century BC. The rock-cut Elephanta Caves were constructed about the mid-5th to 6th centuries AD. The most important among the caves is the great Cave 1, which measures 39 metres from the front entrance to the back. In plan, this cave in the western hill closely resembles Dumar Lena cave at Ellora, in India. The main body of the cave, excluding the porticos on the three open sides and the back aisle, is 27 metres square and is supported by rows of six columns each.

The 7-metre-high masterpiece "Sadashiva" dominates the entrance to Cave 1. The sculpture represents three aspects of Shiva: the Creator, the Preserver, and the Destroyer, identified, respectively, with Aghora or Bhairava (left half), Taptapurusha or Mahadeva (central full face), and Vamadeva or Uma (right half). Representations of Nataraja, Yogishvara, Andhakasuravadha, Ardhanarishwara, Kalyanasundaramurti, Gangadharamurti, and Ravanaanugrahamurti are also noteworthy for their forms, dimensions, themes, representations, content, alignment and execution.

The layout of the caves, including the pillar components, the placement and division of the caves into different parts, and the provision of a sanctum or Garbhagriha of sarvatobhadra plan, are important developments in rock-cut architecture. The Elephanta Caves emerged from a long artistic tradition, but demonstrate refreshing innovation. The combination of aesthetic beauty and sculptural art, replete with respondent Rasas, reached an apogee at the Elephanta Caves. Hindu spiritualistic beliefs and symbology are finely utilized in the overall planning of the caves.

Criteria (i): The fifteen large reliefs surrounding the lingam chapel in the main Elephanta Cave not only constitute one of the greatest examples of Indian art but also one of the most important collections for the cult of Shiva.

Criteria (iii): The caves are the most magnificent achievement in the history of rock-architecture in western India. The Trimurti and other colossal sculptures with their aesthetic setting are examples of unique artistic creation.

Integrity

All the archaeological components in the Elephanta Caves are preserved in their natural settings. There is further scope to reveal archaeological material and enhance information by exposing the buried stupas. At the time of the listing the need was noted to safeguard the fragile site from nearby industrial development. Currently, saline activity and general deterioration of rock surface are affecting the caves. Management of the property would be enhanced through the adoption of a Conservation Management Plan to guide restoration and conservation works.

Authenticity

The authenticity of the property has been well maintained since its inscription on the World Heritage List, despite certain repairs on the façade and pillars that have been carried out to ensure the structural stability of the monument. Besides the caves, Elephanta Island possesses archaeological remains from as early as the 2nd century BC and from the Portuguese period, as witnessed, respectively, by stupas buried towards the eastern side of the hillock and a canon located at its top. Moreover, the caves are preserved in the form of monolithic temples, sarvatobhadra garbhgriha (sanctum), mandapa (courtyard), rock-cut architecture, and sculptures. Since inscription, many interventions have been made to enhance visitors' experience and conserve the site. These include the construction of pathways, conservation of fallen and broken pillars, conservation of fallen and collapsed facades, construction of flight of steps leading to the caves from island's jetty, repair to the Custodian's Quarters, and setting up of a Site Information Centre.

Management and protection requirements

The property is protected primarily by the Archaeological Survey of India, which also undertakes the management of the Elephanta Caves with the assistance of other departments, including the Forest Department, Tourism Department, MMRDA, Urban Development Department, Town Planning Department, and the Gram panchayat of the Government of Maharashtra, all acting under the various legislations of the respective departments, such as the Ancient Monuments and Archaeological Sites and Remains Act (1958) and Rules (1959); Ancient Monuments and Archaeological Sites and Remains (Amendment and Validation) Act (2010); Indian Forest Act (1927), Forest Conservation Act (1980); Municipal Councils, Nagar Panchayats and Industrial Townships Act, Maharashtra (1965); and Regional and Town Planning Act, Maharashtra (1966).

Sustaining the Outstanding Universal Value of the property over time will require completing, approving and implementing a Conservation Management Plan to guide restoration and conservation works; addressing saline activity and the general deterioration of the caves' rock surfaces using internationally recognised scientific standards and techniques; safeguarding the property from nearby industrial development; and considering exposing the buried stupas. The restoration of some pillars carried out in the 1960s must be dismantled and redone as cracks develop. Additional resources (technical specialist advice) and funding are required to conserve this site and protect the archaeology.

V

Golden Temple

The Golden Temple (also known as the Harmandir Sahib, lit. 'abode of God', Punjabi pronunciation: or the Darbār Sahib, 'exalted court', is a gurdwara located in the city of Amritsar, Punjab, India. It is the preeminent spiritual site of Sikhism. It is one of the holiest sites in Sikhism, alongside the Gurdwara Darbar Sahib Kartarpur in Kartarpur, and Gurdwara Janam Asthan in Nankana Sahib.

The man-made pool on the site of the temple was completed by the fourth Sikh Guru, Guru Ram Das, in 1577.In 1604, Guru Arjan Dev, the fifth Sikh Guru, placed a copy of the Adi Granth in Harmandir Sahib and is the prominent figure in development of gurudwara who built it in the 16th Century as per TripClap.The Gurdwara was repeatedly rebuilt by the Sikhs after it became a target of persecution and was destroyed several times by the Mughal and invading Afghan armies. Maharaja Ranjit Singh, after founding the Sikh Empire, rebuilt it in marble and copper in 1809, and overlaid the sanctum with gold leaf in 1830. This has led to the name the Golden Temple.

The Golden Temple is spiritually the most significant shrine in Sikhism. It became a centre of the Singh Sabha Movement between 1883 and 1920s, and the Punjabi Suba movement between 1947 and 1966. In the early 1980s, the Gurdwara became a centre of conflict between the Indian government and a movement led by Jarnail Singh Bhindranwale.In 1984, Prime Minister Indira Gandhi sent in the Indian Army as part of Operation Blue Star, leading to deaths of over 1,000 soldiers and civilians, as well as causing much damage to the Gurdwara and the destruction of Akal Takht. The Gurdwara complex was rebuilt again after the 1984 damage.

The Golden Temple is an open house of worship for all people, from all walks of life and faiths.It has a square plan with four entrances, and a circumambulation path around the pool. The four entrances to the gurudwara symbolises the Sikh belief in equality and the Sikh view that all people are welcome into their holy place.The complex is a collection of buildings around the sanctum and the pool.One of these is Akal Takht, the chief centre of religious authority of Sikhism.Additional buildings include a clock tower, the offices of the Gurdwara Committee, a Museum and a langar – a free Sikh community–run kitchen that offers a vegetarian meal to all visitors without discrimination.Over 150,000 people visit the holy shrine everyday for worship.The Gurdwara complex has been nominated as a UNESCO World Heritage Site, and its application is pending on the tentative list of UNESCO.

Nomenclature

The Harmandir Sahib (Gurmukhi: ਹਰਿਮੰਦਰ ਸਾਹਿਬ) is also spelled as Harimandar or Harimandir Sahib.It is also called the Durbār Sahib (ਦਰਬਾਰ ਸਾਹਿਬ), which means "sacred audience", as well as the Golden Temple for its gold leaf-covered sanctum centre.The word "Harmandir" is composed of two words: "Hari", which scholars translate as "God ", and "mandir", which means "house"."Sahib" is further appended to the shrine's name, the term often used within Sikh tradition to denote respect for places of religious significance.The Sikh tradition has several Gurdwaras named "Harmandir Sahib", such as those in Kiratpur and Patna. Of these, the one in Amritsar is most revered

History

The Golden Temple, Amritsar, c.1840

According to the Sikh historical records, the land that became Amritsar and houses the Harimandir Sahib was chosen by Guru Amar Das, the third Guru of the Sikh tradition. It was then called Guru Da Chakk, after he had asked his disciple Ram Das to find land to start a new town with a man-made pool as its central point. After Guru Ram Das succeeded Guru Amar Das in 1574, and in the face of hostile opposition from the sons of Guru Amar Das,Guru Ram Das founded the town that came to be known as "Ramdaspur". He started by completing the pool with the help of Baba Buddha (not to be confused with the Buddha of Buddhism). Guru Ram Das built his new official centre and home next to it. He invited merchants and artisans from other parts of India to settle in the new town with him.

A Sikh Guru (perhaps Guru Arjan) seated in the Golden Temple at Amritsar in the late 16th or early 17th century, circa 1830 Guler painting

Ramdaspur town expanded during the time of Guru Arjan financed by donations and constructed by voluntary work. The town grew to become the city of Amritsar, and the area grew into the temple complex).The construction activity between 1574 and 1604 is described in Mahima

Prakash Vartak, a semi-historical Sikh hagiography text likely composed in 1741, and the earliest known document dealing with the lives of all the ten Gurus. Guru Arjan installed the scripture of Sikhism inside the new gurdwara in 1604.Continuing the efforts of Guru Ram Das, Guru Arjan established Amritsar as a primary Sikh pilgrimage destination. He wrote a voluminous amount of Sikh scripture including the popular Sukhmani Sahib.

Construction

Maharaja Ranjit Singh listening to Guru Granth Sahib being recited near the Akal Takht and Golden Temple, Amritsar, Punjab, India.

Guru Ram Das acquired the land for the site. Two versions of stories exist on how he acquired this land. In one, based on a Gazetteer record, the land was purchased with Sikh donations of 700 rupees from the people and owners of the village of Tung. In another version, Emperor Akbar is stated to have donated the land to the wife of Guru Ram Das.

In 1581, Guru Arjan initiated the construction of the Gurdwara. During the construction the pool was kept empty and dry. It took 8 years to complete the first version of the Harmandir Sahib. Guru Arjan planned a gurdwara at a level lower than the city to emphasize humility and the need to efface one's ego before entering the premises to meet the Guru. He also demanded that the gurdwara compound be open on all sides to emphasize that it was open to all. The sanctum inside the pool where his Guru seat was, had only one bridge to emphasize that the end goal was one, states Arvind-Pal Singh Mandair. In 1589, the gurdwara made with bricks was complete. Guru Arjan is believed by some later sources to have invited the Sufi saint Mian Mir of Lahore to lay its foundation stone, signalling pluralism and that the Sikh tradition welcomed all. This belief is however unsubstantiated. According to Sikh traditional sources such as Sri Gur Suraj Parkash Granth it was laid by Guru Arjan himself.After the inauguration, the pool was filled with water. On 16 August 1604, Guru Arjan completed expanding and compiling the first version of the Sikh scripture and placed a copy of the Adi Granth in the gurdwara. He appointed Baba Buddha as the first Granthi.

Ath Sath Tirath, which means "shrine of 68 pilgrimages", is a raised canopy on the parkarma (circumambulation marble path around the pool). The name, as stated by W. Owen Cole and other scholars, reflects the belief that visiting this temple is equivalent to 68 Hindu pilgrimage sites in the Indian subcontinent, or that a Tirath to the Golden Temple has the efficacy of all 68 Tiraths combined.The completion of the first version of the Golden Temple was a major milestone for Sikhism, states Arvind-Pal Singh Mandair, because it provided a central pilgrimage place and a rallying point for the Sikh community, set within a hub of trade and activity.

Mughal Empire era destruction and rebuilding

The growing influence and success of Guru Arjan drew the attention of the Mughal Empire. Guru Arjan was arrested under the orders of the Mughal Emperor Jahangir and asked to convert to Islam.He refused, was tortured and executed in 1606 CE. Guru Arjan's son and successor Guru Hargobind left Amritsar and moved into the Shivalik Hills to avoid persecution and to save the Sikh panth. For about a century after Guru Arjan's martyrdom, state Louis E. Fenech and W. H. McLeod, the Golden Temple was not occupied by the actual Sikh Gurus and it remained in hostile sectarian hands.In the 18th century, Guru Gobind Singh and his newly founded Khalsa Sikhs came back and fought to liberate it.The Golden Temple was viewed by the Mughal rulers and Afghan Sultans as the centre of Sikh faith and it remained the main target of persecution.

The Golden Temple was the centre of historic events in Sikh history:

In 1709, the governor of Lahore sent in his army to suppress and prevent the Sikhs from gathering for their festivals of Vaisakhi and Diwali. But the Sikhs defied by gathering in the Golden Temple. In 1716, Banda Singh and numerous Sikhs were arrested and executed.

In 1737, the Mughal governor ordered the capture of the custodian of the Golden Temple named Mani Singh and executed him. He appointed Masse Khan as the police commissioner who then occupied the Temple and converted it into his entertainment centre with dancing girls. He befouled the pool. Sikhs avenged the sacrilege of the Golden Temple by assassinating Masse Khan inside the Temple in August 1740.

In 1746, another Lahore official Diwan Lakhpat Rai working for Yahiya Khan, and seeking revenge for the death of his brother, filled the pool with sand. In 1749, Sikhs restored the pool when Muin ul-Mulk slackened Mughal operations against Sikhs and sought their help during his operations in Multan.

In 1757, the Afghan ruler Ahmad Shah Durrani, also known as Ahmad Shah Abdali, attacked Amritsar and desecrated the Golden Temple. He had waste poured into the pool along with entrails of slaughtered cows, before departing for Afghanistan. The Sikhs restored it again.

In 1762, Ahmad Shah Durrani returned and had the Golden Temple blown up with gunpowder. Sikhs returned and celebrated Diwali in its premises. In 1764, Baba Jassa Singh Ahluwalia collected donations to rebuild the Golden

Temple. A new main gateway (Darshan Deorhi), causeway and sanctum were completed in 1776, while the floor around the pool was completed in 1784. The Sikhs also completed a canal to bring in fresh water from Ravi River for the pool.

Shri Harmandir Sahib was attacked by the Afghan forces under Ahmed Shah Abdali in December,1,1764. Baba Gurbaksh Singh along with 29 other Sikhs lead a last stand against the much larger Afghan forces and were killed in the skirmish. Abdali then destroyed Shri Harmandir Sahib for the 3rd time.

RANJEET SINGH RECONSTRUCTION

Ranjit Singh founded the nucleus of the Sikh Empire at the age of 36 with help of Sukerchakia Misl forces he inherited and those of his mother-in-law Rani Sada Kaur. In 1802, at age 22, he took Amritsar from the Bhangi Sikh misl, paid homage at the Golden Temple and announced that he would renovate and rebuild it with marble and gold. The Temple was renovated in marble and copper in 1809, and in 1830 Ranjit Singh donated gold to overlay the sanctum with gold leaf.

After learning of the Gurdwara through Maharaja Ranjit Singh,the 7th Nizam of Hyderabad "Mir Osman Ali Khan" started giving yearly grants towards it.

The management and operation of Durbar Sahib – a term that refers to the entire Golden Temple complex of buildings, was taken over by Ranjit Singh. He appointed Sardar Desa Singh Majithia (1768–1832) to manage it and made land grants whose collected revenue was assigned to pay for the Temple's maintenance and operation. Ranjit Singh also made the position of Temple officials hereditary.

Destruction and reconstruction after Indian independence

Interior of Darbar Sahib with gold encrusted walls and featuring a golden chandelier

The destruction of the temple occurred during the Operation Blue Star. It was the codename of an Indian military action carried out between 1 and 8 June 1984 to remove militant Sikh Jarnail Singh Bhindranwale and his followers from the buildings of the Harmandir Sahib (Golden Temple) complex in Amritsar, Punjab. The decision to launch the attack rested with Prime Minister Indira Gandhi. In July 1982, Harchand Singh Longowal, the President of the Sikh political party Akali Dal, had invited Bhindranwale to take up residence in the Golden Temple Complex to evade arrest. The government claimed Bhindranwale later made the sacred temple complex an armoury and headquarters.

On 1 June 1984, after negotiations with the militants failed, Indira Gandhi ordered the army to launch Operation Blue Star, simultaneously attacking scores of Sikh temples across Punjab.A variety of army units and paramilitary forces surrounded the Golden Temple complex on 3 June 1984. The fighting started on 5 June with skirmishes and the battle went on for three days, ending on 8 June. A clean-up operation codenamed Operation Woodrose was also initiated throughout Punjab.

The army had underestimated the firepower possessed by the militants, whose armament included Chinese-made rocket-propelled grenade launchers with armour piercing capabilities. Tanks and heavy artillery were used to attack the militants, who responded with anti-tank and machine-gun fire from the heavily fortified Akal Takht. After a 24-hour firefight, the army gained control of the temple complex. Casualty figures for the army were 83 dead and 249 injured. According to the official estimates, 1,592 militants were apprehended and there were 493 combined militant and civilian casualties.According to the government claims, high civilian casualties were attributed to militants using pilgrims trapped inside the temple as human shields.

Brahma Chellaney, the Associated Press's South Asia correspondent, was the only foreign reporter who managed to stay on in Amritsar despite the media blackout.His dispatches, filed by telex, provided the first non-governmental news reports on the bloody operation in Amritsar. His first dispatch, front-paged by The New York Times, The Times of London and The Guardian, reported a death toll about twice of what authorities had admitted. According to the dispatch, about 780 militants and civilians and 400 troops had perished in fierce gun-battles.Chellaney reported that about "eight to ten" men suspected Sikh militants had been shot with their hands tied. In that dispatch, Mr. Chellaney interviewed a doctor who said he had been picked up by the army and forced to conduct postmortems despite the fact he had never done any postmortem examination before. In reaction to the dispatch, the Indian government charged Chellaney with violating Punjab press censorship, two counts of fanning sectarian hatred and trouble, and later with sedition,calling his report baseless and disputing his casualty figures.

The military action in the temple complex was criticized by Sikhs worldwide, who interpreted it as an assault on the Sikh religion. Many Sikh soldiers in the army deserted their units;several Sikhs resigned from civil administrative office and returned awards received from the Indian government. Five months after the operation, on 31 October 1984, Indira Gandhi was assassinated in an act of revenge by her two Sikh bodyguards, Satwant Singh and Beant Singh.Public outcry over Gandhi's death led to the killings of more than 3,000 Sikhs in Delhi alone, in the ensuing 1984 anti-Sikh riots.

In December 2021, a young man was allegedly beaten to death after disrupting the Rehras Sahib (evening prayer) at the sanctum of the temple. He reportedly jumped over a railing and picked up the sword lying before the temple's copy of the Guru Granth Sahib, before attempting to touch the Guru Granth Sahib itself. He was subsequently overpowered by the sangat and received fatal injuries to the head.

Architecture

The Golden Temple's architecture reflects different architectural practices prevalent in the Indian subcontinent, as various iterations of temple were rebuilt and restored. The Temple is described by Ian Kerr, and other scholars, as a mixture of the Indo-Islamic Mughal and the Hindu Rajput architecture.

The sanctum is a 12.25 x 12.25 metre square with two storeys and a gold leaf dome. This sanctum has a marble platform that is a 19.7 x 19.7 metre square. It sits inside an almost square (154.5 x 148.5 m2) pool called amritsar or amritsarovar (amrit means nectar, sar is short form of sarovar and means pool). The pool is 5.1 metre deep and is surrounded by a 3.7 metre wide circumambulatory marble passage that is circled clockwise. The sanctum is connected to the platform by a causeway and the gateway into the causeway is called the Darshani Ḍeorhi (from Darshana Dvara). For those who wish to take a dip in the pool, the Temple provides a half hexagonal shelter and holy steps to Har ki Pauri.Bathing in the pool is believed by many Sikhs to have restorative powers, purifying one's karma. Some carry bottles of the pool water home particularly for sick friends and relatives. The pool is maintained by volunteers who perform kar seva (community service) by draining and desilting it periodically.

The sanctum has two floors. The Sikh Scripture Guru Granth Sahib is seated on the lower square floor for about 20 hours every day, and for 4 hours it is taken to its bedroom inside Akal Takht with elaborate ceremonies in a palki, for sukhasana and Prakash. The floor with the seated scripture is raised a few steps above the entrance causeway level. The upper floor in the sanctum is a gallery and connected by stairs. The ground floor is lined with white marble, as is the path surrounding the sanctum. The sanctum's exterior has gilded copper plates. The doors are gold leaf-covered copper sheets with nature motifs such as birds and flowers. The ceiling of the upper floor is gilded, embossed and decorated with jewels. The sanctum dome is semi-spherical with a pinnacle ornament. The sides are embellished with arched copings and small solid domes, the corners adorning cupolas, all of which are covered with gold leaf-covered gilded copper.

The floral designs on the marble panels of the walls around the sanctum are Arabesque. The arches include verses from the Sikh scripture in gold letters. The frescoes follow the Indian tradition and include animal, bird and nature motifs rather than being purely geometrical. The stair walls have murals of Sikh Gurus such as the falcon carrying Guru Gobind Singh riding a horse.

The Darshani Deorhi is a two-storey structure that houses the temple management offices and treasury. At the exit of the path leading away from the sanctum is the Prasada facility, where volunteers serve a flour-based sweet offering called Karah prasad. Typically, the pilgrims to the Golden Temple enter and make a clockwise circumambulation around the pool before entering the sanctum. There are four entrances to the gurdwara complex signifying the openness to all sides, but a single entrance to the sanctum of the temple through a causeway.

They also have free service of wheelchair. Anyone can take wheelchair and roam around the temple. Worshipper can take wheelchair from starting entrance and they have a special lift to physically challenged people.

: Jallianwala Bagh massacre

As per tradition, the Sikhs gathered in the Golden Temple to celebrate the festival of Baisakhi in 1919. After their visit, many walked over to the Jallianwala Bagh next to it to listen to speakers protesting Rowlatt Act and other policies implemented by the British colonial government. A large crowd had gathered, when Colonel Reginald Edward Harry Dyer ordered a detachment of ninety soldiers (drawn from the 9th Gorkha Rifles and the 59th Scinde Rifles) under his command to surround the Jallianwala Bagh, and then open fire into the crowd. 379 were killed and thousands were wounded in the massacre. The massacre strengthened the opposition to colonial rule throughout India, particularly that from Sikhs. It triggered massive non-violent protests. The protests pressured the British colonial government to transfer the control over the management and treasury of the Golden Temple to an elected organisation called Shiromani Gurudwara Prabandhak Committee (SGPC). The SGPC continues to manage the Golden Temple.

Punjabi Suba movement

The Punjabi Suba movement was a long-drawn political agitation, launched by the Sikhs, demanding the creation of a Punjabi Suba, or Punjabi-speaking state, in the post-independence state of East Punjab.[100] It was first presented as a policy position in April 1948 by the Shiromani Akali Dal,after the States Reorganization Commission set up after independence was not effective in the north of the country during its work to delineate states on a linguistic basis. The Golden Temple complex was the main centre of operations of the movement, and important events during the movement that occurred at the gurdwara included the 1955 raid by the government to quash the movement, and the subsequent Amritsar Convention in 1955 to convey Sikh sentiments to the central government.The complex was also the site of speeches, demonstrations, and mass arrests, and where leaders of the movement domiciled in huts during hunger strikes.The borders of the modern state of Punjab, along with the official status of the state's native language of Punjabi in the Gurmukhi script, are the result of the movement, which culminated in the setting of the current borders in 1966.

VI

Amber Fort

Amer Fort or Amber Fort is a fort located in Amer, Rajasthan, India. Amer is a town with an area of 4 square kilometres (1.5 sq mi) located 11 kilometres (6.8 mi) from Jaipur, the capital of Rajasthan. Amber city and Amber fort were founded by ruler Alan Singh of Chanda dynasty of Meenas.Located high on a hill, it is the principal tourist attraction in Jaipur. Amer Fort is known for its artistic style elements. With its large ramparts and series of gates and cobbled paths, the fort overlooks Maota Lake, which is the main source of water for the Amer Palace.

Amer Palace is great example of Rajput architecture. Some of its buildings and work have influence of Mughal architecture. Constructed of red sandstone and marble, the attractive, opulent palace is laid out on four levels, each with a courtyard. It consists of the Diwan-e-Aam, or "Hall of Public Audience", the Diwan-e-Khas, or "Hall of Private Audience", the Sheesh Mahal (mirror palace), or Jai Mandir, and the Sukh Niwas where a cool climate is artificially created by winds that blow over a water cascade within the palace. Hence, the Amer Fort is also popularly known as the

Amer Palace. The palace was the residence of the Rajput Maharajas and their families. At the entrance to the palace near the fort's Ganesh Gate, there is a temple dedicated to Shila Devi, a Goddess of the Chaitanya cult, which was given to Raja Man Singh when he defeated the Raja of Jessore, Bengal in 1604. (Jessore is now in Bangladesh).Raja Man Singh had 12 queens so he made 12 rooms, one for each Queen. Each room had a staircase connected to the King's room but the Queens were not to go upstairs. Raja Jai Singh had only one queen so he built one room equal to three old queen's rooms.

This palace, along with Jaigarh Fort, is located immediately above on the Cheel ka Teela (Hill of Eagles) of the same Aravalli range of hills. The palace and Jaigarh Fort are considered one complex, as the two are connected by a subterranean passage. This passage was meant as an escape route in times of war to enable the royal family members and others in the Amer Fort to shift to the more redoubtable Jaigarh Fort. Annual tourist visitation to the Amer Palace was reported by the Superintendent of the Department of Archaeology and Museums as 5000 visitors a day, with 1.4 million visitors during 2007. At the 37th session of the World Heritage Committee held in Phnom Penh, Cambodia, in 2013, Amer Fort, along with five other forts of Rajasthan, was declared a UNESCO World Heritage Site as part of the group Hill Forts of Rajasthan.

Geography

Amer Palace is situated on a forested hill promontory that juts into Maota Lake near the town of Amer, about 11 kilometres (6.8 mi) from Jaipur city, the capital of Rajasthan. The palace is near National Highway 11C to Delhi. A narrow 4WD road leads up to the entrance gate, known as the Suraj Pol (Sun Gate) of the fort. It is now considered much more ethical for tourists to take jeep rides up to the fort, instead of riding the elephants.

History

Amber was a Meena state, Which was ruled by his Susawat clan. After defeating whom Kakil Deo, son of Dulherai, made Amber the capital of Dhundhar after Khoh.

The state of Jaipur was earlier known as Amber or Dhundhar and was controlled by Meena chiefs of five different tribes who were under suzerainty of the Bargurjar Rajput Raja of Deoti. Later a Kachhwaha prince Dulha Rai destroyed the sovereignty of Meenas and also defeated Bargurjars of Deoli and took Dhundhar fully under Kachwaha rule.

The Amber Fort were originally built by Raja Man Singh. Jai Singh I expanded it. Improvements and additions were done successive rulers over the next 150 years, until the Kachwahas shifted their capital to Jaipur during the time of Sawai Jai Singh II, in 1727. Amer was known in the medieval period as Dhundar (meaning attributed to a sacrificial mount in the western frontiers) and ruled by the Kachwahas from the 11th century onwards – between 1037 and 1727 AD, till the capital was moved from Amer to Jaipur.The history of Amer is indelibly linked to these rulers as they founded their empire at Amer.

Magic flower

A particular attraction here is the "magic flower" carved marble panel at the base of one of the pillars around the mirror palace depicting two hovering butterflies; the flower has seven unique designs including a fishtail, lotus, hooded cobra, elephant trunk, lion's tail, cob of corn, and scorpion, each one of which is visible by a special way of partially hiding the panel with the hands.

Garden

The garden, located between the Jai Mandir on the east and the Sukh Niwas on the west, both built on high platforms in the third courtyard, was built by Mirza Raja Jai Singh (1623–68). It is patterned on the lines of the Chahar Bagh or Mughal Garden. It is in a sunken bed, shaped in a hexagonal design. It is laid out with narrow channels lined with marble around a star-shaped pool with a fountain at the center. Water for the garden flows in cascades through channels from the Sukh Niwas and also from the cascade channels called the "chini khana niches" that originate on the terrace of the Jai Mandir.

Tripolia gate

Tripolia gate means three gates. It is access to the palace from the west. It opens in three directions, one to the Jaleb Chowk, another to the Man Singh Palace and the third one to the Zenana Deorhi on the south.

Lion gate

The Lion Gate, the premier gate, was once a guarded gate; it leads to the private quarters in the palace premises and is titled 'Lion Gate' to suggest strength. Built during the reign of Sawai Jai Singh (1699–1743 AD), it is covered with frescoes; its alignment is zigzag, probably made so from security considerations to attack intruders.

Conservation

Six forts of Rajasthan, namely, Amber Fort, Chittor Fort, Gagron Fort, Jaisalmer Fort, Kumbhalgarh and Ranthambore Fort were included in the UNESCO World Heritage Site list during the 37th meeting of the World Heritage Committee in Phnom Penh during June 2013. They were recognized as a serial cultural property and examples of Rajput military hill architecture.

The town of Amer, which is an integral and inevitable entry point to Amer Palace, is now a heritage town with its economy dependent on the large influx of tourists (4,000 to 5,000 a day during peak tourist season). This town is spread over an area of 4 square kilometres (1.5 sq mi) and has eighteen temples, three Jain mandirs, and three mosques. It has been listed by the World Monument Fund (WMF) as one of the 100 endangered sites in the world; funds for conservation are provided by the Robert Wilson Challenge Grant.As of 2005, some 87 elephants lived within the fort grounds, but several were said to be suffering from malnutrition.

Conservation works have been undertaken at the Amer Palace grounds at a cost of Rs 40 crores (US$8.88 million) by the Amer Development and Management Authority (ADMA). However, these renovation works have been a subject of intense debate and criticism with respect to their suitability to maintain and retain the historicity and architectural features of the ancient structures. Another issue which has been raised is the commercialization of the place.

A film unit shooting a film at the Amer Fort damaged a 500-year-old canopy, demolished the old limestone roof of Chand Mahal, drilled holes to fix sets and spread large quantities of sand in Jaleb Chowk in utter disregard and violation of the Rajasthan Monuments, Archaeological Sites and Antique Act (1961).The Jaipur Bench of the Rajasthan High Court intervened and stopped the film shooting with the observation that "unfortunately, not only the public but especially the concerned (sic) authorities have become blind, deaf and dumb by the glitter of money. Such historical protected monuments have become a source of income."

Concerns of elephant abuse

Several groups have raised concerns regarding the abuse of elephants and their trafficking and have highlighted what some consider the inhumane practice of riding elephants up to the Amber Palace complex.The organization PETA as well as the central zoo authority have taken up this serious issue. The Haathi gaon (Elephant village) is said to be in violation of captive animal controls, and a PETA team found elephants chained with painful spikes, blind, sick and injured elephants forced to work, and elephants with mutilated tusks and ears.In 2017, A New York-based tour operator announced it would use Jeeps instead of elephants for the trip to Amber Fort, saying "It's not worth endorsing ... some really significant mistreatment of animals."

VII

Agra Fort

The Agra Fort is a historical fort in the city of Agra in India also known as the Red Fort. Built by the Mughal emperor Akbar in 1565 and completed in 1573, it served as the main residence of the rulers of the Mughal Dynasty until 1638, when the capital was shifted from Agra to Delhi. It was also known as the "Lal-Qila", "Fort Rouge" or "Qila-i-Akbari". Before capture by the British, the last Indian rulers to have occupied it were the Marathas. In 1983, the Agra fort was life inscribed as a UNESCO World Heritage Site. It is about 2.5 km northwest of its more famous sister monument, the Taj Mahal. The fort can be more accurately described as a walled city.

Like the rest of Agra, the history of Agra Fort prior to Mahmud Ghaznavi's invasion is unclear. However, in the 15th century, the Chauhan Rajputs occupied it. Soon after, Agra assumed the status of capital when Sikandar Lodi (A.D. 1487–1517) shifted his capital from Delhi and constructed a few buildings in the pre-existing fort at Agra. After the first battle of Panipat (A.D. 1526) Mughals captured the fort and ruled from it. In A.D. 1530, Humayun was crowned in it. The fort was given its present appearance during the reign of Akbar (A.D. 1556–1605). Later this fort was under the rule of Jats of Bharatpur for 13 years.

History

After the First Battle of Panipat in 1526, Babur stayed in the fort, in the palace of Ibrahim Lodi. He later built a baoli (step well) in it. His successor, Humayun, was crowned in the fort in 1530. He was defeated at Bilgram in 1540 by Sher Shah Suri. The fort remained with the Suris till 1555, when Humayun recaptured it. Adil Shah Suri's general, Hemu, recaptured Agra in 1556 and pursued its fleeing governor to Delhi where he met the Mughals in the Battle of Tughlaqabad.

Realising the importance of its central situation, Akbar made it his capital and arrived in Agra in 1558. His historian, Abul Fazl, recorded that this was a brick fort known as 'Badalgarh'. It was in a ruined condition and Akbar had it rebuilt with red sandstone from Barauli area Dhaulpur district, in Rajasthan.Architects laid the foundation and it was built with bricks in the inner core with sandstone on external surfaces. Some 4,000 builders worked on it daily for eight years, completing it in 1573.

It was only during the reign of Akbar's grandson, Shah Jahan, that the site took on its current state. Shah Jahan built the beautiful Taj Mahal in the memory of his wife, Mumtaz Mahal. Unlike his grandfather, Shah Jahan tended to have buildings made from white marble.

The fort was under the Jat rulers of Bharatpur for 13 years. In the fort, they built the 'Ratan Singh ki Haveli'. The fort was invaded and captured by the Maratha Empire in the early 18th century. Thereafter, it changed hands between the Marathas and their foes many times. After their catastrophic defeat at Third Battle of Panipat by Ahmad

Shah Abdali in 1761, Marathas remained out of the region for the next decade. Finally Mahadji Shinde took the fort in 1785. It was lost by the Marathas to the British during the Second Anglo-Maratha War in 1803. The fort was the site of a battle during the Indian rebellion of 1857 which caused the end of the British East India Company's rule in India and led to a century of direct rule in India by Britain.

On 30 November 1871, thirty six people died when a cartridge factory located inside the fort exploded.

Layout

The 380,000 m2 (94-acre) fort has a semicircular plan, its chord lies parallel to the river Yamuna and its walls are seventy feet high. Double ramparts have massive circular bastions at intervals, with battlements, embrasures, machicolations and string courses. Four gates were provided on its four sides, one Khizri gate opening on to the river. Two of the fort's gates are notable: the "Delhi Gate" and the "Lahore Gate." The Lahore Gate is also popularly also known as the "Amar Singh Gate," for Amar Singh Rathore.

The monumental Delhi Gate, which faces the city on the western side of the fort, is considered the grandest of the four gates and a masterpiece of Akbar's time. It was built circa 1568 both to enhance security and as the king's formal gate, and includes features related to both. It is embellished with intricate inlay work in white marble. A wooden drawbridge was used to cross the moat and reach the gate from the mainland; inside, an inner gateway called Hathi Pol ("Elephant Gate") – guarded by two life-sized stone elephants with their riders – added another layer of security. The drawbridge, slight ascent, and 90-degree turn between the outer and inner gates make the entrance impregnable. During a siege, attackers would employ elephants to crush a fort's gates. Without a level, straight run-up to gather speed, however, that is prevented by this layout.

Because the Indian military (the Parachute Brigade in particular) is still using the northern portion of the Agra Fort, the Delhi Gate cannot be used by the public. Tourists enter via the Amar Singh Gate.

The site is very important in terms of architectural history. Abul Fazal recorded that five hundred buildings in the beautiful designs of Bengal and Gujarat were built in the fort. Some of them were demolished by Shah Jahan to make way for his white marble palaces. Most of the others were destroyed by the British troops of East India Company between 1803 and 1862 for raising barracks. Hardly thirty Mughal buildings have survived on the south-eastern side, facing the river, such as the Delhi Gate and Akbar Gate and one palace – "Bengali Mahal".

Akbar Darwazza (Akbar Gate) was renamed Amar Singh Gate by Shah Jahan. The gate is similar in design to the Delhi Gate. Both are built of red sandstone.

The Bengali Mahal is built of red sandstone and is now split into Akbari Mahal and Jahangiri Mahal.

Jahangir's Hauz (tank) A.D. 1610: This monolithic tank (hauz) was used for bathing. It is 5 feet high, 8 feet in diameter and 25 feet in circumference. On the external side of the rim there is an inscription in Persian which mentions it as 'Hauz-e-Jahangir'. It was first discovered near the courtyard of Akbar's palace. In A.D. 1843 and later it was placed in front of Diwan-e-Am. In 1862, it was shifted to public garden (Company Bagh) where it suffered much damage. Later, Sir John Marshall brought it back to Agra Fort and placed there. Due to this hauz, the palace became famous as Jahangiri Mahal though it is part of Akbar's

Bengali mahal.

Shahjahani Mahal (1628-35 A.D.): It is situated in between the white marble Khas Mahal and the red stone Jahangiri Mahal and is set transitionally in between these two residential complexes of two different ages. It is the earliest attempt of the Mughal emperor Shahjahan to convert an existing red stone building in accordance with his taste and it was his earliest palace in Agra Fort. It has a large hall, side rooms and an octagonal tower on the riverside. The skeletal construction of brick and red stone was all redone with a thick white stucco plaster and colourfully painted in floral designs. The whole palace once glistened white like white marble. On the face towards the Khas Mahal, is a large spacious white marble dalan, composed of five arches, supported on double pillars and protected externally by a chhajja. Its closed western bay houses, the Ghaznin gate, Babur's baoli and a well are situated beneath it.

The Ghaznin Gate, taken in 1842 from the tomb of Mahmud of Ghazni in Ghazni, Afghanistan.

Ghaznin Gate (1030 A.D.): The gate originally belonged to the tomb of Mahmud Ghaznavi at Ghazni. It was brought from there by the British in1842. Lord Ellenborough, the Governor General, in historic proclamation claimed, that these were the sandalwood gates of Somnath which Mahmud had taken to Ghazni in 1025, and the British had thus avenged an insult of 800 years back. This false claim was made just to win the goodwill of the Indian people. The gate is, in fact, made of local deodar wood of Ghazni and not of sandalwood. The style of decoration bears no resemblance to ancient Gujrati woodwork. There is also an Arabic inscription carved on the upper part. It mentions Mahmud with his epithets. Sir John Marshall had placed here a notice-board which described the whole episode about this gate. It is 16.5 feet high and 13.5 feet broad and its wight is about half a ton. It is made up of geometrical, hexagonal and octagonal panels which have been fixed, one with the help of the other into the frame without rivets. The idea to restore it at Somnath was ultimately given up and the gate was abandoned. Since then, it is stored in a room.

Jahangir's Chain of Justice (C. 1605 A.D.): This is the spot where Mughal king Jahangir instituted his 'chain of justice'(Zanjir-i-Adl) in c. 1605 A.D. He records in his memoir that after his accession, the first order he gave, "was for the fastening up of the chain of justice so that if those engaged in the administration of justice should delay or practice hypocrisy, the aggrieved might come to this chain and shake it so that its noise might attract my attention." It was made of pure gold. It was 80' in length and had 60 bells. Its weight was 1 Quintal. One end was fastened to the battlements of the Shah-Burj and the other end to a stone post on the bank of the river. This is not a myth. Contemporary foreign travellers like William Hawkins personally saw it. It has also been depicted in a contemporary painting made in 1620 A.D. This was a way to redress the grievances of the people who could approach the king, the highest judicial authority of the empire, directly, without fee, fear or formality for immediate relief. There was no distinction of caste or creed or between poor and rich. Jahangir's administration of justice 'Adl-i-Jahangir' became a legend in Indian history.

The Muthamman Burj (Shah-Burj) & Jharokha (1632 -1640 A.D.): This beautiful palace surmounts the largest bastion of Agra Fort on the riverside, facing the East. It was originally built of red stone by Akbar who used it for jharokha darshan, as well as for sun worship, every day at sunrise. Jehangir also used it as jharokha, as is faithfully shown in his painting made in 1620. He also instituted his 'Adl-i-Janjir'(the chain of justice) on its south side. Owing to its octagonal plan, it was called 'Muthamman Burj'. It has also been mentioned as 'Shah-Burj'(the imperial or king's tower) by Persian historians and foreign travellers. Its name jasmine tower or 'Samman-Burj' as recorded by the contemporary historian Lahauri is a misnomer. It was rebuilt with white marble by Shah Jehan around 1632-1640 A.D. He also used it for jharokha darshan which was an indispensable a Mughal institution as was 'Durbar'. It is an octagonal building, five external sides of which make a dalan overlooking the river. Each side has pillar and bracket openings, the easternmost side projects forward and accommodates a jharokha majestically. On the western side of this palace is a spacious dalan with Shah-Nasin (alcoves). A shallow water-basin (kunda) is sunk in its pavement. It is profusely inlaid. This dalan opens on a court which has a chabutara projected by a jali screen, on its northern side, a series of rooms leading to Shish Mahal on its western side; and a colonnade (dalan) with a room attached to its on the southern side. It is, thus, a large complex entirely built of white marble. It has deep niches on the walls, to break the monotony. Dados have repetitive stylized creepers inlaid on borders and carved plants on the centre pillars, brackets and lintels also bear exquisitely inlaid designs and it is one of the most ornamented buildings of Shah Jehan. This palace is directly connected to the Diwan-i-Khas, Shish Mahal, Khas Mahal, and other palaces. and it was from here that the Mughal emperor governed the whole country. This burj offers full and majestic view of Taj Mahal and Shah Jehan spent eight years (1658-1666 A.D.) of his imprisonment in this complex, and it is said that he died here. His body was taken by boat to the Taj Mahal and buried.

Shish Mahal (A.D. 1631–40): It was built by Mughal Emperor Shahjahan as a part of summer palace. Its most distinctive feature is glass mosaic work done on its walls and ceiling. These glass pieces have high mirror quality which glittered and twinkled in thousand ways in semi-dark interior. The glass was imported from Haleb of Syria. Shahjahan built glass palace also at Lahore and Delhi.

VIII

Sun Temple

Konark Sun Temple is a 13th-century CE (year 1250) Sun temple at Konark about 35 kilometres (22 mi) northeast from Puri city on the coastline in Puri district, Odisha, India. The temple is attributed to king Narasimhadeva I of the Eastern Ganga dynasty about 1250 CE.

Dedicated to the Hindu Sun God Surya, what remains of the temple complex has the appearance of a 100-foot (30 m) high chariot with immense wheels and horses, all carved from stone. Once over 200 feet (61 m) high,much of the temple is now in ruins, in particular the large shikara tower over the sanctuary; at one time this rose much higher than the mandapa that remains. The structures and elements that have survived are famed for their intricate artwork, iconography, and themes, including erotic kama and mithuna scenes. Also called the Surya Devalaya, it is a classic illustration of the Odisha style of Architecture or Kalinga architecture.

The cause of the destruction of the Konark temple is unclear and still remains a source of controversy.Theories range from natural damage to deliberate destruction of the temple in the course of being sacked several times by Muslim armies between the 15th and 17th centuries.This temple was called the "Black Pagoda" in European sailor accounts as early as 1676 because it looked like a great tiered tower which appeared black. Similarly, the Jagannath Temple in Puri was called the "White Pagoda". Both temples served as important landmarks for sailors in the Bay of Bengal.The temple that exists today was partially restored by the conservation efforts of British India-era archaeological teams. Declared a UNESCO world heritage site in 1984,it remains a major pilgrimage site for Hindus, who gather here every year for the Chandrabhaga Mela around the month of February.

Konark Sun Temple is depicted on the reverse side of the Indian currency note of 10 rupees to signify its importance to Indian cultural heritage.

The walls of the temple from the temple's base through the crowning elements are ornamented with reliefs, many finished to jewelry-quality miniature details. The terraces contain stone statues of male and female musicians holding various musical instruments including the vina, mardala, gini,Other major works of art include sculptures of Hindu deities, apsaras and images from the daily life and culture of the people (artha and dharma scenes), various animals, aquatic creatures, birds, legendary creatures, and friezes narrating the Hindu texts. The carvings include purely decorative geometric patterns and plant motifs. Some panels show images from the life of the king such as one showing him receiving counsel from a guru, where the artists symbolically portrayed the king as much smaller than the guru, with the king's sword resting on the ground next to him.

The upana (moulding) layer at the bottom of the platform contains friezes of elephants, marching soldiers, musicians, and images depicting the secular life of the people, including hunting scenes, a caravan of domesticated animals, people carrying supplies on their head or with the help of a bullock cart, travelers preparing a meal along the roadside, and festive processions.On other walls are found images depicting the daily life of the elite as well as the common people. For example, girls are shown wringing their wet hair, standing by a tree, looking from a window, playing with pets, putting on makeup while looking into a mirror, playing musical instruments such as the vina, chasing away a monkey who is trying to snatch items, a family taking leave of their elderly grandmother who seems dressed for a pilgrimage, a mother blessing her son, a teacher with students, a yogi during a standing asana, a warrior being greeted with a namaste, a mother with her child, an old woman with a walking stick and a bowl in her hands, comical characters, among others.

The Konark temple is also known for its erotic sculptures of maithunas.These show couples in various stages of courtship and intimacy, and in some cases coital themes. Notorious in the colonial era for their uninhibited celebration of sexuality, these images are included with other aspects of human life as well as deities that are typically associated with tantra. This led some to propose that the erotic sculptures are linked to the vama marga (left hand tantra) tradition. However, this is not supported by local literary sources, and these images may be the same kama and mithuna scenes found integrated into the art of many Hindu temples. The erotic sculptures are found on the temple's Shikhara, and these illustrate all the bandhas (mudra forms) described in the Kamasutra.

Other large sculptures were a part of the gateways of the temple complex. These include life-size lions subduing elephants, elephants subduing demons, and horses. A major pillar dedicated to Aruna, called the Aruna Stambha, used to stand in front of the eastern stairs of the porch. This, too, was intricately carved with horizontal friezes and motifs. It now stands in front of the Jagannatha temple at Puri.

History

Konark, also referred to in Indian texts by the name Kainapara, was a significant trading port by the early centuries of the common era. The current Konark temple dates to the 13th century, though evidence suggests that a sun temple was built in the Konark area by at least the 9th century.Several Puranas mention Surya worship centers in Mundira, which may have been the earlier name for Konark, Kalapriya (Mathura), and Multan (now in Pakistan).The Chinese Buddhist pilgrim and traveler

According to the Madala Panji, there was at one time another temple in the region built by Pundara Kesari. He may have been Puranjaya, the 7th-century ruler of the Somavamshi dynasty.

Cultural significance

Religion is frequently at the centre of the Odia (previously Orissan) cultural expression, and Konark occupies an important space in it as part of The Golden Triangle (Jagannath Temple, Puri, and the Lingaraja Temple of Bhubaneswar completing it) which represents the pinnacle of Odia (previously Orissan) masonry and temple architecture.

Literature

Numerous poems, stories, and novels have been written about Konark, most of which explore or expand or reinterpret the tragedies inherent in the legends and stories about the temple. Most recently, Mohanjit's book of poems, Kone Da Suraj, which revolves around Konark, won the Kendra Sahitya Academy Award (one of the top awards for literature in India) for Punjabi language.

IX

Khajuraho Group Of Monuments

The Khajuraho Group of Monuments are a group of Hindu and Jain temples in Chhatarpur district, Madhya Pradesh, India. They are about 175 kilometers southeast of Jhansi, 10km from Azad Nagar Khajwa, 9km from Rajnagar and 49 km from district headquarter Chhatarpur. They are a UNESCO World Heritage Site.The temples are famous for their nagara-style architectural symbolism and a few erotic sculptures.

Most Khajuraho temples were built between 885 AD and 1000 AD by the Chandela dynasty.Historical records note that the Khajuraho temple site had 85 temples by the 12th century, spread over 20 square kilometers. Of these, only about 25 temples have survived, spread over six square kilometers. Of the surviving temples, the Kandariya Mahadeva Temple is decorated with a profusion of sculptures with intricate details, symbolism and expressiveness of ancient Indian art. The temple complex was forgotten and overgrown by the jungle until 1838 when Captain T.S. Burt, a British engineer, visited the complex and reported his findings in the Journal of the Asiatic Society of Bengal.

When these monuments were built, the boys in the place lived in hermitages, by being brahmcharis (bachelor) until they attained manhood and these sculptures helped them to learn about the worldly role of 'householder'. The Khajuraho group of temples were built together but were dedicated to two religions, Hinduism and Jainism, suggesting a tradition of acceptance and respect for diverse religious views among Hindus and Jains in the region.

Location

The Khajuraho monuments are located in the Indian state of Madhya Pradesh, in Chatarpur district, about 620 kilometres (385 mi) southeast of New Delhi. The temples are located near a small town also known as Khajuraho, with a population of about 24,481 people (2011 Census).

Khajuraho is served by Civil Aerodrome Khajuraho (IATA Code: HJR), with services to Delhi, Agra, Varanasi and Mumbai.The site is also linked by the Indian Railways service, with the railway station located approximately six kilometres from the entrance to the monuments.

The monuments are about ten kilometres off the east-west National Highway 75, and about 50 kilometres from the city of Chhatarpur, which is connected to the state capital Bhopal by the SW-NE running National Highway 86.

The 10th-century Bhand Deva Temple in Rajasthan was built in the style of the Khajuraho monuments and is often referred to as 'Little Khajuraho'.

History

The Khajuraho group of monuments was built during the rule of the Chandela dynasty. The building activity started almost immediately after the rise of their power, throughout their kingdom to be later known as Bundelkhand. Most temples were built during the reigns of the Hindu kings Yashovarman and Dhanga. Yashovarman's legacy is best exhibited by the Lakshmana Temple. Vishvanatha temple best highlights King Dhanga's reign. The largest and currently most famous surviving temple is Kandariya Mahadeva built in the reign of King Vidyadhara.The temple inscriptions suggest many of the currently surviving temples were complete between 970 and 1030 AD, with further temples completed during the following decades.

The Khajuraho temples were built about 35 miles from the medieval city of Mahoba,the capital of the Chandela dynasty, in the Kalinjar region. In ancient and medieval literature, their kingdom has been referred to as Jijhoti, Jejahoti, Chih-chi-to and Jejakabhukti.

The first documented mention of Khajuraho was made in 641 by Xuanzang, a Chinese pilgrim who described encountering several dozen inactive Buddhist monasteries and a dozen Hindu temples with a thousand worshipping brahmins. In 1022 CE, Khajuraho was mentioned by Abu Rihan-al-Biruni, the Persian historian who accompanied Mahmud of Ghazni in his raid of Kalinjar; he mentions Khajuraho as the capital of Jajahuti. The raid was unsuccessful, and a peace accord was reached when the Hindu king agreed to pay a ransom to Mahmud of Ghazni to end the attack and leave.

Khajuraho temples were in active use through the end of the 12th century. This changed in the 13th century; after the army of Delhi Sultanate, under the command of the Muslim Sultan Qutb-ud-din Aibak, attacked and seized the Chandela kingdom. About a century later, Ibn Battuta, the

Moroccan traveller in his memoirs about his stay in India from 1335 to 1342 AD, mentioned visiting Khajuraho temples, calling them "Kajarra"as follows:

Until the 12th century, Khajuraho was under Hindu kings and featured 85 temples. Central India was seized by Delhi Sultanate in the 13th century. Under Muslim rule, many temples were destroyed and the rest left in neglect. Ruins of some old temples (Ghantai temple above) are still visible.

...near (Khajuraho) temples, which contain idols that have been mutilated by the Moslems, live a number of yogis whose matted locks have grown as long as their bodies. And on account of extreme asceticism they are all yellow in colour. Many Moslems attend these men in order to take lessons (yoga) from them.

— Ibn Battuta, about 1335 AD, Riḥlat Ibn Baṭūṭah, Translated by Arthur Cotterell

The central Indian region, where Khajuraho temples are, was controlled by various Muslim dynasties from the 13th century through the 18th century. In this period, some temples were desecrated, followed by a long period when they were left in neglect.In 1495 AD, for example, Sikandar Lodi's campaign of temple destruction included Khajuraho. The remoteness and isolation of Khajuraho protected the Hindu and Jain temples from continued destruction by Muslims. Over the centuries, vegetation and forests overgrew the temples.

In the 1830s, local Hindus guided a British surveyor, T.S. Burt, to the temples and they were thus rediscovered by the global audience. Alexander Cunningham later reported, few years after the rediscovery, that the temples were secretly in use by yogis and thousands of Hindus would arrive for pilgrimage during Shivaratri celebrated annually in February or March based on a lunar calendar. In 1852,

F.C. Maisey prepared earliest drawings of the Khajuraho temples.

The temple site is within Vindhya mountain range in central India. An ancient local legend held that Hindu deity Shiva and other gods enjoyed visiting the dramatic hill formation in Kalinjar area.The center of this region is Khajuraho, set midst local hills and rivers. The temple complex reflects the ancient Hindu tradition of building temples where gods love to pray.

The temples are clustered near water, another typical feature of Hindu temples. The current water bodies include Sib Sagar, Khajur Sagar (also called Ninora Tal) and Khudar Nadi (river).Local legends state that the temple complex had 64 water bodies, of which 56 have been physically identified by archeologists so far.

All temples, except one (Chaturbhuja) face the sunrise – another symbolic feature that is predominant in Hindu temples. The relative layout of temples integrate masculine and feminine deities and symbols highlight the interdependence. The artworks symbolically highlight the four goals of life considered necessary and proper in Hinduism – dharma, kama, artha and moksha.

Of the surviving temples, six are dedicated to Shiva, eight to Vishnu and his affinities, one to Ganesha, one to Sun god, three to Jain Tirthankars.For some ruins, there is insufficient evidence to assign the temple to specific deities with confidence.

An overall examination of site suggests that the Hindu symbolic mandala design principle of square and circles is present each temple plan and design. Further, the territory is laid out in three triangles that converge to form a pentagon. Scholars suggest that this reflects the Hindu symbolism for three realms or trilokinatha, and five cosmic substances or panchbhuteshvara.The temple site highlights Shiva, the one who destroys and recycles life, thereby controlling the cosmic dance of time, evolution and dissolution.

The temples have a rich display of intricately carved statues. While they are famous for their erotic sculpture, sexual themes cover less than 10% of the temple sculpture. Further, most erotic scene panels are neither prominent nor emphasized at the expense of the rest, rather they are in proportional balance with the non-sexual images. The viewer has to look closely to find them, or be directed by a guide. The arts cover numerous aspects of human life and values considered important in the Hindu pantheon. Further, the images are arranged in a configuration to express central ideas of Hinduism. All three ideas from Āgamas are richly expressed in Khajuraho temples – Avyakta, Vyaktavyakta and Vyakta.

The Beejamandal temple is under excavation. It has been identified with the Vaidyanath temple mentioned in the Grahpati Kokalla inscription.

Of all temples, the Matangeshvara temple remains an active site of worship. It is another square grid temple, with a large 2.5 metres (8.2 ft) high and 1.1 metres (3.6 ft) diameter lingam, placed on a 7.6 metres (25 ft) diameter platform.

The most visited temple, Kandariya Mahadev, has an area of about 6,500 square feet and a shikhara (spire) that rises 116 feet

X

Akshardham Temple

Swaminarayan Akshardham is a Hindu temple, and spiritual-cultural campus in Delhi, India. The temple is close to the border with Noida. Also referred to as Akshardham Temple or Akshardham Delhi, the complex displays millennia of traditional and modern Hindu culture, spirituality, and architecture. Inspired by Yogiji Maharaj and created by Pramukh Swami Maharaj, it was constructed by BAPS.

The temple was officially opened on 6 November 2005 by Pramukh Swami Maharaj in the presence of Dr. A. P. J. Abdul Kalam, Manmohan Singh, L.K Advani and B.L Joshi. The temple, at the centre of the complex, was built according to the Vastu shastra and Pancharatra shastra.

In Swaminarayan Akshardham, similar to its predecessor Swaminarayan Akshardham in Gandhinagar, Gujarat, the main shrine is the focal point and maintains the central position of the entire complex. There are various exhibition halls which provide information about the life and work of Swaminarayan. The designers of the complex have adopted contemporary modes of communication and technology to create the various exhibition halls.

The complex features an abhishek mandap, Sahaj Anand water show, a thematic garden, and three exhibitions namely Sahajanand Darshan (Hall of Values), Neelkanth Darshan (an IMAX film on the early life of Swaminarayan as the teenage yogi, Neelkanth), and Sanskruti Darshan (cultural boat ride). According to Swaminarayan Hinduism, the word Akshardham means the abode of Swaminarayan and believed by followers as a temporal home of God on earth.

Akshardham Mandir

The main attraction of the Swaminarayan Akshardham complex is the Akshardham Mandir. It rises 141-foot (43 m) high, spans 316-foot (96 m) wide, and extends 356-foot (109 m) long. It is intricately carved with flora, fauna, dancers, musicians, and deities.

The Akshardham Mandir was designed by BAPS Swamis and Virendra Trivedi, a member of the Sompura family.It is entirely constructed from Rajasthani pink sandstone and Italian Carrara marble. Based on traditional Hindu architectural guidelines (Shilpa shastras) on maximum temple life span, it makes no use of ferrous metal. Thus, it has no support from steel or concrete.

The mandir also consists of 234 ornately carved pillars, nine domes, and 20,000 murtis of swamis, devotees, and acharyas. The mandir also features the Gajendra Pith at its base, a plinth paying tribute to the elephant for its importance in Hindu culture and India's history. It contains 148 life sized elephants in total weighing a total of 3000 tons.

Under the temple's central dome lies the 11-foot (3.4m) high murti of Swaminarayan seated in abhayamudra to whom the temple is dedicated. Swaminarayan is surrounded by images of the faith's lineage of Gurus depicted either in a devotional posture or in a posture of service. Each murti is made of paanch dhaatu or five metals in accordance to Hindu tradition. The temple also houses the murtis of Sita Ram, Radha Krishna, Shiv Parvati, and Lakshmi Narayan.

Exhibits

Sahajanand Darshan [Hall of Values]

The Hall of Values features lifelike robotics and dioramas which display incidents from Swaminarayan's life, portraying his message about the importance of peace, harmony, humility, service to others and devotion to God. Set in 18th century India, the audience experiences eternal messages gleaned from ancient Hindu culture such as non-violence, vegetarianism, perseverance, prayers, morality, and family harmony through 15 3-dimensional dioramas which make use of state of the art robotics, fibre optics, light and sound effects, dialogues, and music. The hall also features the world's smallest animatronic robot in the form of Ghanshyam Maharaj, the child form of Swaminarayan.

Nilkanth Darshan [Theatre]

The theatre houses Delhi's first and only large format screen, measuring 85-foot (26 m) by 65-foot (20 m). The theatre shows a 40-minute film specially commissioned for the complex, Neelkanth Yatra, to recount a seven-year pilgrimage made by Swaminarayan made during his teenage years throughout India. Mystic India, an international version of the film produced by BAPS Charities, was released in 2005 at IMAX theatres and giant screen cinemas worldwide. A 27-foot (8.2 m) tall bronze murti of Neelkanth Varni is located outside the theatre.

Sanskruti Vihar [Boat Ride]

The Boat Ride is a 12-minute journey through 10,000 years glorious heritage, using life size figures and robotics to depict life in Vedic India, from family life to bazaars and teaching.It also shows the contributions of Vedic Indians to various fields such as science, astronomy, arts, literature, yoga, mathematics, etc. by eminent persons like mathematician-astronomers Aryabhata and Brahmagupta, grammarian Pāṇini, contributors to the ancient art and science of Ayurveda like Sushruta and Charaka, Classical Sanskrit writer Kālidāsa, philosopher, economist and royal advisor Chanakya, among others. It shows the world's first university, Takshashila and the subjects taught there such as horse riding and warfare. It moves on to the Middle Ages to Sufi saints like Kabir and saints from the Bhakti movement such as Meera and Ramananda and then to recent times highlighting the contributions of modern Indian mathematicians such as Jagadish Chandra Bose, Srinivasa Ramanujan, C. V. Raman and Satyendra Nath Bose and philosophers like Swami Vivekananda.

XI

Gwalior Fort

The Gwalior Fort commonly known as the Gwāliiyar Qila, is a hill fort near Gwalior, Madhya Pradesh, India. The fort has existed at least since the 10th century, and the inscriptions and monuments found within what is now the fort campus indicate that it may have existed as early as the beginning of the 6th century. The modern-day fort, embodying a defensive structure and two palaces was built by the Tomar Rajput ruler Man Singh Tomar. The fort has been administered by a number of different rulers in its history.

The present-day fort consists of a defensive structure and two main palaces, "Man Mandir" and Gujari Mahal, built by Tomar Rajput ruler Man Singh Tomar (reigned 1486–1516 CE), the latter one for his wife, Queen Mrignayani.The second oldest record of "zero" in the world was found in a small temple (the stone inscription has the second oldest record of the numeric zero symbol having a place value as in the modern decimal notation), which is located on the way to the top. The inscription is around 1500 years old

The word Gwalior is derived from one of the names for Gwalipa. According to legend, Gwalipa cured the local chieftain Suraj Sen of leprosy, and in gratitude, Suraj Sen founded the city of Gwalior in his name.

Topography

The fort is built on an outcrop of Vindhyan sandstone on a solitary rocky hill called Gopachal. This feature is long, thin, and steep. The geology of the Gwalior range rock formations is ochre coloured sandstone covered with basalt. There is a horizontal stratum, 342 feet (104 m) at its highest point (length 1.5 miles (2.4 km) and average width 1,000 yards (910 m)). The stratum forms a near-perpendicular precipice. A small river, the Swarnrekha, flows close to the palace.

History

Courtyard of Maan Mandir

The exact period of Gwalior Fort's construction is uncertain. According to a local legend, the fort was built by a local king named Suraj Sen in 3 CE. He was cured of leprosy, when a sage named Gwalipa offered him the water from a sacred pond, which now lies within the fort. The grateful king constructed a fort, and named it after the sage. The sage bestowed the title Pal ("protector") upon the king, and told him that the fort would remain in his family's possession, as long as they bear this title. 83 descendants of Suraj Sen Pal controlled the fort, but the 84th, named Tej Karan, lost it.

The inscriptions and monuments found within what is now the fort campus indicate that it may have existed as early as the beginning of the 6th century.A Gwalior inscription describes a sun temple built during the reign of the Huna emperor Mihirakula in 6th century. The Teli ka Mandir, now located within the fort, was built by the

Gurjara-Pratiharas in the 9th century.

The fort definitely existed by the 10th century, when it is first mentioned in the historical records. The Kachchhapaghatas controlled the fort at that time, most probably as feudatories of the Chandelas. From 11th century onwards, the Muslim dynasties attacked the fort several times. In 1022 CE, Mahmud of Ghazni besieged the fort for four days. According to Tabaqat-i-Akbari, he lifted the siege in return for a tribute of 35 elephants. Bahauddin Tourghil a senior slave of the Ghurid ruler Muhammad of Ghor captured the fort in 1196 after a long siege.The Delhi Sultanate lost the fort for a short period before it was recaptured by Iltutmish in 1232 CE.

In 1398, the fort came under the control of the Tomars. The most distinguished of the Tomar rulers was Maan Singh, who commissioned several monuments within the fort. The Delhi Sultan Sikander Lodi tried to capture the fort in 1505 but was unsuccessful. Another attack, by his son Ibrahim Lodi in 1516, resulted in Maan Singh's death. The Tomars ultimately surrendered the fort to the Delhi Sultanate after a year-long siege.

Gwalior Fort was the base for many of Hemu's campaigns.

Within a decade, the Mughal Emperor Babur captured the fort from the Delhi Sultanate. The Mughals lost the fort to Sher Shah Suri in 1542. Afterwards, the fort was captured and used by Hemu, the Hindu general and, later, the last Hindu ruler of Delhi, as his base for his many campaigns, but Babur's grandson Akbar recaptured it in 1558. Akbar made the fort a prison for political prisoners. For example, Abul-Kasim,son of Kamran and Akbar's first cousin was held and executed at the fort. The last Tomar king of Gwalior, Maharaja Ramshah Tanwar, who had then taken refuge in Mewar and had fought at the Battle of Haldighati. He was martyred in the battle along with his three sons (which included Shalivahan Singh Tomar, the heir-apparent)

Guru Hargobind, on 24 June 1606, at age 11, was crowned as the sixth Sikh Guru. At his succession ceremony, he put on two swords: one indicated his spiritual authority (piri) and the other, his temporal authority (miri).Because of the execution of Guru Arjan by Mughal Emperor Jahangir, Guru Hargobind from the very start was a dedicated enemy of the Mughal rule. He advised the Sikhs to arm themselves and fight.The death of his father at the hands of Jahangir prompted him to emphasise the military dimension of the Sikh community.[18] Jahangir responded by jailing the 14 year old Guru Hargobind at Gwalior Fort in 1609, on the pretext that the fine imposed on Guru Arjan had not been paid by the Sikhs and Guru Hargobind. It is not clear as to how much time he spent as a prisoner. The year of his release appears to have been either 1611 or 1612, when Guru Hargobind was about 16 years old.Persian records, such as Dabistan i Mazahib suggest he was kept in jail for twelve years, including over 1617–1619 in Gwalior, after which he and his camp were kept under Muslim army's surveillance by Jahangir. According to Sikh tradition, Guru Hargobind was released from the bondage of prison on Diwali. This important event in Sikh history is now termed the Bandi Chhor Divas festival.

Aurangzeb's brother, Murad Bakhsh and nephew Sulaiman Shikoh were also executed at the fort. The killings took place in the Man Mandir palace. Sipihr Shikoh was imprisoned at Gwalior Fort from 1659 to 1675. Aurangzeb's son, Muhammad Sultan was imprisoned at the fort from January 1661 to December 1672. After the death of

Aurangzeb, the Jat ruler of Gohad Bhim Singh Rana seized the Gwalior Fort in the Battle of Gwalior. The Marathas had captured many territories held by the declining Mughal Empire in Northern and Central India after the death of Aurangzeb. The Maratha incursions into North India were raids by the Peshwa Bajirao. in 1755-1756, The Marathas took over Gwalior fort by defeating the Jat ruler of Gohad. The Maratha general Mahadaji Shinde (Scindia) captured the fort from the Gohad Rana Chhatar Singh, but later lost it to the British East India Company. On August 3, 1780, a Company force under Captains Popham and Bruce captured the fort in a nighttime raid, scaling the walls with 12 grenadiers and 30 sepoys. Both sides suffered fewer than 20 wounded total. In 1780, the British governor Warren Hastings restored the fort to the Ranas of Gohad. The Marathas recaptured the fort four years later, and this time the British did not intervene because the Ranas of Gohad had become hostile to them. Daulat Rao Sindhia lost the fort to the British during the Second Anglo-Maratha War.

There were frequent changes in the control of the fort between the Scindias and the British between 1808 and 1844. In January 1844, after the battle of Maharajpur, the fort was occupied by the Gwalior State of the Maratha Scindia family, as a protectorate of the British government.[13]:69 During the 1857 uprising, around 6500 sepoys stationed at Gwalior rebelled against the Company rule, although the company's vassal ruler Jayajirao Scindia remained loyal to the British. The British took control of the fort in June 1858. They rewarded Jayajirao with some territory but retained control of the Gwalior Fort. By 1886, the British were in complete control of India, and the fort no longer had any strategic importance to them. Therefore, they handed over the fort to the Scindia family. The

Maratha Scindias continued to rule Gwalior until the independence of India in 1947, and built several monuments including the Jai Vilas Mahal.

XII

Mahabodhi Temple

The Mahabodhi Temple (literally: "Great Awakening Temple") or the Mahābodhi Mahāvihāra, a UNESCO World Heritage Site, is an ancient, but rebuilt and restored Buddhist temple in Bodh Gaya, Bihar, India, marking the location where the Buddha is said to have attained enlightenment. Bodh Gaya is 15 km from Gaya and is about 96 km (60 mi) from Patna.

The site contains a descendant of the Bodhi Tree under which Buddha gained enlightenment, and has been a major pilgrimage destination of Buddhists for well over two thousand years, and some elements date to the period of Ashoka (died c. 232 BCE). What is now visible on the ground essentially dates from the 5th century CE, or possibly earlier, as well as several major restorations since the 19th century. But the structure now may well incorporate large parts of earlier work, possibly from the 2nd or 3rd century CE.Archaeological finds from the site however, indicate that the place was a site of veneration for Buddhists since at least the Mauryan period. In particular, the Vajrasana, which is located within the temple itself has been dated to the third century BCE.

Many of the oldest sculptural elements have been moved to the museum beside the temple, and some, such as the carved stone railing wall around the main structure, have been replaced by replicas. The main temple's survival is especially impressive, as it was mostly made of brick covered with stucco, materials that are much less durable than stone. However, it is understood that very little of the original sculptural decoration has survived.

The temple complex includes two large straight-sided shikhara towers, the largest over 55 metres (180 feet) high. This is a stylistic feature that has continued in Jain and Hindu temples to the present day, and influenced Buddhist architecture in other countries, in forms like the pagoda.

The Buddha

Ashoka's Mahabodhi Temple and Diamond throne in Bodh Gaya, built c. 250 BCE. The inscription between the Chaitya arches reads: "Bhagavato Sakamunino/ bodho" i.e. "The building round the Bodhi tree of the Bhagavat(Holy) Sakamuni (Shakyamuni)". Also interesting to note is the word Bhagavā for Buddha is used in Buddhist texts.The elephant-crowned pillar of Ashoka (now lost) is visible. Bharhut frieze (c. 100 BCE).

Traditional accounts say that, around 589 BCE,Siddhartha Gautama, a young prince who saw the suffering of the world and wanted to end it, reached the forested banks of the Phalgu river, near the city of Gaya, India. There he sat in meditation under a peepul tree (Ficus religiosa or Sacred Fig) which later became known as the Bodhi tree. According to Buddhist scriptures, after three days and three nights, Siddharta attained enlightenment and the answers that he had sought. In that location, Mahabodhi Temple was built by Emperor Ashoka in around

260 BCE.

The Buddha then spent the succeeding seven weeks at seven different spots in the vicinity meditating and considering his experience. Several specific places at the current Mahabodhi Temple relate to the traditions surrounding these seven weeks:

The first week was spent under the Bodhi tree.

During the second week, the Buddha remained standing and stared, uninterrupted, at the Bodhi tree. This spot is marked by the Animeshlocha Stupa, that is, the unblinking stupa or shrine, to the north-east of the Mahabodhi Temple complex. There stands a statue of Buddha with his eyes fixed towards the Bodhi tree.

The Buddha is said to have walked back and forth between the location of the Animeshlocha Stupa and the Bodhi tree. According to legend, lotus flowers sprung up along this route; it is now called Ratnachakrama or the jewel walk.

He spent the fourth week near Ratnagar Chaitya, to the north-east side.

He spent the sixth week next to the Lotus pond.

He spent the seventh week under the Rajyatna tree.

The Bodhi tree at Bodhgaya is directly connected to the life of the historical Buddha, Siddhartha Gautama, who attained enlightenment or omniscient wisdom when he was meditating under it. The temple was built directly to the east of the Bodhi tree, supposedly a direct descendant of the original Bodhi Tree.

According to Buddhist mythology, if no Bodhi tree grows at the site, the ground around the Bodhi tree is devoid of all plants for a distance of one royal karīsa. Through the ground around the Bodhi tree no being, not even an elephant, can travel.

According to the Jatakas, the navel of the earth lies at this spot,and no other place can support the weight of the Buddha's attainment. Another Buddhist tradition claims that when the world is destroyed at the end of a kalpa, the Bodhimanda is the last spot to disappear, and will be the first to appear when the world emerges into existence again. Tradition also claims that a lotus will bloom there, and if a Buddha is born during the new kalpa, the lotus flowers in accordance with the number of Buddhas expected to arise.According to legend, in the case of Gautama Buddha, a Bodhi tree sprang up on the day he was born

In approximately 250 BCE, about 200 years after the Buddha attained enlightenment, Emperor Ashoka of the Mauryan Empire visited Bodh Gaya in order to establish a monastery and shrine on the holy site, which have today disappeared.

There remains however the Diamond throne, which he had established at the foot of the Bodhi tree. The Diamond throne, or Vajrasana, is thought to have been built by Emperor Ashoka of the Maurya Empire between 250 and 233 BCE,. at the location where the Buddha reached enlightenment. It is worshiped today, and is the center of many festivities at the temple.

Representations of the early temple structure meant to protect the Bodhi tree are found at Sanchi, on the toraṇas of Stūpa I, dating from around 25 BCE, and on a relief carving from the stupa railing at Bhārhut, from the early Shunga period (c. 185–c. 73 BCE).

Sunga structures

Reconstitution of the Sunga period pillars at Bodh Gaya, from archaeology (left) and from artistic relief (right). They are dated to the 1st century BCE. Reconstitution done by

Alexander Cunningham.[17]

Columns with pot-shaped bases

Additional structures were brought in by the Sungas. In particular, columns with pot-shaped bases were found around the Diamond throne. These columns are thought to date to the 1st century BCE, towards the end of the Sungas. These columns, which were found through archaeological research at the Buddha's Walk in the Mahabodhi Temple, quite precisely match the columns described on the reliefs found on the gateway pillars.

Buddhism declined when the dynasties patronizing it declined, following Huna invasions and the early Arab Islamic invasions such as that of Muhammad bin Qasim. A strong revival occurred under the Pala Empire in the northeast of the subcontinent (where the temple is situated). Mahayana Buddhism flourished under the Palas between the 8th and the 12th century. However, after the defeat of the Palas by the Sena dynasty, Buddhism's position again began to erode and became nearly extinct in India. During the 12th century CE, Bodh Gaya and the nearby regions were invaded by Muslim Turk armies, led by Delhi Sultanate's Qutb al-Din Aibak and Bakhtiyar Khilji. During this period, the Mahabodhi Temple fell into disrepair and was largely abandoned. The last abbot of the Mahabodhi temple was Sariputra, who left India and travelled to Nepal in the 15th century. Over the following centuries, the monastery's abbot or mahant position became occupied by the area's primary landholder, who claimed ownership of the Mahabodhi Temple grounds.

In the 13th century, Burmese Buddhists built a temple with the same name and modelled on the original Mahabodhi Temple

Restoration

During the 13th century and again the 19th century, Burmese rulers undertook restoration of the temple complex and surrounding wall. In the 1880s, the then-British colonial government of India began to restore Mahabodhi Temple under the direction of Sir Alexander Cunningham and Joseph David Beglar. In 1884, a large Buddha image of the Pāla period, likely removed at an earlier stage to the Mahant's residence from the temple sanctum, was reinstated.The plith of the image was reconstructed at the time and parts of the dedicatory inscription inserted in their current position.The inscription records the rededication of the image by Pīṭhīpati Jayasena in the 13th century. In 1886, Sir Edwin Arnold visited the site and under guidance from Ven. Weligama Sri Sumangala published several articles drawing the attention of the Buddhists to the deplorable conditions of Buddhagaya.The sculpture has since been repaired, painted and gilded and is under active worship in the sanctum.

Recent events

In 2013, the upper portion of the temple was covered with 289 kg of gold. The gold was a gift from the King of Thailand and devotees from Thailand, and installed with the approval of the Archaeological Survey of India.

2013 attack

: 2013 Bodh Gaya blasts

On 7 July 2013, ten low-intensity bombs exploded in the temple complex, injuring 5 people. One bomb was near the statue of Buddha and another was near the Mahabodhi tree. Three unexploded bombs were also found and defused. The blasts took place between 5.30 a.m. and 6.00 a.m.The main temple was undamaged. The Intelligence Bureau of India may have alerted state officials of possible threats around 15 days prior to the bombing.On 4 November 2013, the National Investigation Agency announced that the Islamic terrorist group Indian Mujahideen was responsible for the bombings

XIII

Tirupati

Tirupati is a city in the Indian state of Andhra Pradesh. It is the administrative headquarters of the Tirupati district. The city is home to the important Hindu shrine of Tirumala Venkateswara Temple and other historic temples and is referred to as the "Spiritual Capital of Andhra Pradesh".It is located at a distance of 150 km from Chennai, 250 km from Bangalore and 750 km from Vishakhapatnam. It is one of the eight Swayam vyaktha kshetras (Self-Manifested Temples) dedicated to Vishnu. Tirupati is a municipal corporation and the headquarters of Tirupati (urban) mandal, Tirupati (rural) mandal, and the Tirupati revenue division.

It is the 7th most urban agglomerated city in the state, with a population of 459,985 in 2011 and around 1,004,615 in 2021. As of 2011 census, it had a population of 287,035 making it the 9th most populous city in Andhra Pradesh. It is the second biggest city in Rayalaseema after Kurnool. For the year 2012–2013, India's Ministry of Tourism named Tirupati as the "Best Heritage City". Tirupati has been selected as one of the hundred Indian cities to be developed as a smart city under Smart Cities Mission by Government of India.

Etymology

In Dravidian languages and especially in Tamil, tiru is an honorific that means sacred. Pati means abode. Tirupati (Tirumala) is referred to as Pushpa-mandapa in Acharya-Hridayam (13th century).

History

Puranas

According to Varaha Purana, during Treta Yuga, Rama resided here along with Sita and Lakshmana on his return from Lankapuri.

As per the Purana, a loan of one crore and 11.4 million gold coins was sought by Balaji from Kubera for his marriage with Padmavathi. To pay back the loan, devotees from all over India visit the temple and donate money.

Ancient history

Tirupati was developed by Pallava Kings from 6th century onwards. The city became a great Vaishnava centre during the time of Ramanujacharya in 11th century, from where Srivaishnavism spread to other parts of Andhra Desa. Srikurmam Temple in Srikakulam district of Andhra Pradesh bears the inscription saying Tirupati Srivaishnavula Raksha.Tirupati survived the Muslim invasions by accepting to pay Jizya to the Muslims. During the early 1300s Muslim invasion of South India, the deity of Sri Ranganathaswamy Temple, Srirangam was brought to Tirupati for safekeeping.

The temple town for most of the medieval era part of Vijayanagara Empire until the 17th century and its rulers contributed considerable resources and wealth notable by Krishna Deva Raya and Achyuta Deva Raya, Sadasiva Raya and Tirumala Deva Raya.

The city has many historical temples including the Venkateswara Temple which bears 1,150 inscriptions in the Sanskrit, Tamil, Telugu and Kannada languages.Out of 1150 inscriptions 236 belong to Pallava, Chola and Pandya dynasties, 169 belonged to Saluva dynasty, 251 belonged to Achyuta Deva Raya period, 130 belonged to Sadasiva Raya period and another 135 originated in Aravidu dynasty. which specify the contributions of the Pallava Kingdom around the ninth century CE, Chola Kingdom around the tenth century CE and the Vijayanagara Empire in the 14th century CE.During the 15th century, Sri Tallapaka Annamacharya sung many songs in praise of the holy town in Telugu. He compared it to be divine, including the rocks, streams, trees, animals, and adds that it is heaven on the earth. One example of such a song is:

Tirumala, in all its right, is heaven. Its powers are indescribable. The Vedas have taken the form of rocks and appeared on Tirumala. Holiness has taken the form of water and is flowing as streams on Tirumala. Its holy peaks are Brahmaloka and other lokas. Srinivasa lives on Seshadri.

There was no human settlement at Lower Tirupati until 1500. With the growing importance of Upper Tirupati, a village formed at the present-day Kapilatheertham Road area and was named "kotturu". It was later shifted to the vicinity of Govindarajaswamy Temple which was consecrated around the year 1130 CE. Later the village grew into its present-day form around Govindaraja Swamy Temple which is now the heart of the city. It has now gained a lot of popularity as a tourism place

Printed by Libri Plureos GmbH in Hamburg,
Germany